Praise for *Walk Through This*

"Sara is a woman of great passion, courage, joy, and adventure—and all of those qualities make her the perfect person to share hope with others who have experienced the trauma of great betrayal. She uses her story to help others chart a path for their own journey of healing and growth. If you have been betrayed and wonder if anything can ever feel alive again, Sara's story and process not only will lead you to restoration but also will encourage you to become who you were always meant to be!"

—Dr. Barbara Steffens, LPCC, coauthor of *Your Sexually Addicted Spouse* and founding/retired president of Association of Partners of Sex Addicts Trauma Specialists (APSATS)

"This book is a warm companion on the journey through the wild of forgiveness. Sara's words are filled with insight and encouragement, as you walk through this journey called life, breath by breath, step by step."

—Morgan Harper Nichols, artist, poet, and bestselling author of *All Along You Were Blooming: Thoughts for Boundless Living*

"Sara's story is one of deep trauma and betrayal but also profound healing and releasing. Through her own deep self-healing work, she is able to mirror to us all the beautiful ways we were created to heal."

—Ruthie Lindsey, speaker and author of *There I Am: The Journey from Hopelessness to Healing*

"In *Walk Through This*, Schulting Kranz has written a brave and helpful book about the undersung power of nature, adventure, and forgiveness for healing trauma. I hope it will inspire many people to head outside, together."

—Florence Williams, journalist and author of *The Nature Fix: Why Nature Makes Us Happier, Healthier, and More Creative*

"This redefinition of forgiveness is needed now more than ever before. The collapse of spring 2020 has made it clear that trauma is part of being human. Through her remarkable and shocking story, Sara's experience and strength illuminate how a forgiveness practice is a beautiful tool for transformation and being truly *alive*. Since reading this book, I've seen my life through a new lens—past, present and future. Though I've lived in the jungle for over a decade, this was a profound reminder of Mother Nature's healing power. Sara's natural and unconventional, yet practical, approach resonates deeply with me. *Walk Through This* definitely won't be collecting dust on my shelf! I'll be returning to this resource frequently and passing its wisdom on to my children, as we all learn how to let go of negative feelings, practice kindness to ourselves (and others!), and create a better world."

—Tamara Jacobi, author of *Wildpreneurs: A Practical Guide to Pursuing Your Passion as a Business*

"Sara's story charts a journey that begins with a shocking revelation, then weathers loss, self-doubt, and despair, to arrive at self-acceptance and the ultimate goal: forgiveness. Her inspiring path provides detailed directions for charting one's own way to salvation. Sara is a beautiful example of how one can truly save herself."

—Laura VanZee Taylor, writer/director of the documentary *I Am Maris*

Walk Through This

HARNESS THE HEALING POWER OF NATURE AND TRAVEL THE ROAD TO FORGIVENESS

SARA SCHULTING KRANZ

HARPER
HORIZON

Published by Harper Horizon, an imprint of HarperCollins Focus LLC.

Any internet addresses, phone numbers, or company or product information
printed in this book are offered as a resource and are not intended in any
way to be or to imply an endorsement by Harper Horizon, nor does Harper
Horizon vouch for the existence, content, or services of these sites, phone
numbers, companies, or products beyond the life of this book.

ISBN 978-0-7852-3866-9 (eBook)
ISBN 978-0-7852-3865-2 (HC)

Library of Congress Cataloging-in-Publication Data

Library of Congress Control Number: 2020938624

Printed in the United States of America

20 21 22 23 LSC 10 9 8 7 6 5 4 3 2 1

To my three sons: Jacob, Carson, and Christian.
You are my truth, inspiration, and hope.
You are my heroes.

Contents

Introduction

When I was eighteen years old, a loving voice in my head shared a message: *Sara, you were handed this life for a reason. No one should go through what you have. Someday you will write a book and give hope to others so they don't feel alone. Stay courageous and strong.*

Perhaps it was God, spirit, my inner warrior, or ancestors from long ago seeing my internal struggle during a traumatic time—and what was possible if provided the opportunity to speak my truth. I tucked the message in my heart and silently carried on as a young mom and full-time college student. Soon I became a wife, teacher, and mother to three boys. We moved across the country and experienced big life changes, but every so often I remembered those words and wondered why the time never felt right to pursue what I knew would someday happen.

At the age of forty, the delay made sense when so much of what I thought to be true about my life turned out to be a lie. And here we are today.

Life Doesn't Happen on Our Time

Letting go of how I thought my life would unfold has been the hardest lesson and biggest struggle for someone who is a former control seeker. As a young girl born into a family that lived a simple, happy life in a Midwest village and farming community, I was led to believe my journey would somehow be perfectly mapped out. I thought I'd be married to a man who would love me unconditionally and we would grow old together. I'd be a mom to three or four kids, make cookies surrounded by family at the holidays, and have a home where every child on the block would feel welcomed.

Sounds lovely, right?

It does, but that's not at all what happened.

Here's what did. And though it's not all pretty, I'll spare the suspense and tell you that I've never been happier! I've made a commitment to embrace and learn from every experience in my life: good, difficult, or otherwise. My relationship with my internal self and the universe (to me known as God, spirit, love, nature, ancestors, or higher consciousness) is stronger than ever—and because of that I wouldn't change one detail of what has led me to where I am today.

At the age of seventeen, a year before receiving the loving message about writing this book, I experienced my first major trauma. It happened at a friend's house as we watched *Saturday Night Live*. He wanted to have sex.

"Come on. It's no big deal," he said.

I said no, but he wouldn't listen. He demanded and forced himself on me. I was sexually assaulted by this "friend," someone I'd thought I could trust.

I stood in the bathroom, desperately trying to clean off what had happened. Catching my eyes in the mirror between wipes, I wanted to cry but couldn't. I felt numb and angry. To have your body used for another person's gain creates unimaginable tragedy and loss.

Before that night, I was an outgoing, athletic young girl with a bright future. Afterward, I was terrified and confused, and my ability to trust was stripped away. As the days went on, I convinced myself to "let it go" and pretend it didn't happen. To face what happened hurt too much.

But a few weeks later, I missed my period.

I can't be pregnant. Sitting alone in my bathroom, I took a test and prayed for a negative result.

Both lines turned blue.

Lying on the floor of my parents' home, I curled up in a ball and sobbed. *Why . . . why?* Repercussions from that night were like a nightmare that didn't end.

My school was small and everyone knew one another, making what happened more difficult. I struggled with shame, remorse, and responsibility. The police refused to press charges, citing insufficient evidence. I wasn't believed.

"You shouldn't have been at the house alone."

"You should have screamed."

"Are you sure you didn't want to?"

Questioning from authorities, social workers, doctors, and my community was unbearable, all while I sought a restraining order for my rapist, who continued to stalk me.

To this day, I struggle with my memory of the evening. Details are fragmented and incomplete. For decades, the "not remembering," mixed with others' judgments, made me wonder if it was all my fault. How do you come to terms with what happened when your brain won't provide details but your body remembers dissociating because of fear? The court system and society rely on details and proof. Sadly, neither cared about my growing belly and invisible scars.

My parents were in their own pain and sought to protect me. They found a counselor through Catholic Social Services, someone trustworthy who they were told could help. There were so many choices to make, including if I should abort the baby. I have the utmost respect for my parents as they left this decision to me, because it was my body and a choice I would need to carry for a lifetime. Knowing the magnitude of this decision was huge. No words can describe the unexplainable energy and strong pull from my womb that triggered my choice to go through with the pregnancy.

Giving birth at seventeen years old was lonely. Mom never left my side, but I didn't have a partner to look after me or wipe my brow. So many things went wrong. From thirty-six hours in labor to an ineffective epidural, it was not a pleasant experience. But seeing this child for the first time made all of the pain wash away. He was pure love, magnified innocence, and beautiful. I believe he was heaven sent regardless of how he was brought into the world, this little angel who became mine.

"Go check on my baby, please. He's crying." My brother quickly found out the strength of a mother and child's bond. Looking confused, he got up from the chair across from my hospital bed and said, "But he's down the hall in the nursery. How do you know?" He went to the nursery, then returned in amazement. "Wow, Sara. You were right. The nurse is taking care of him. That's so cool!"

We question others when we don't agree with their choices. How much kinder would this world be if we could set aside our own judgments and realize no two life journeys are alike? I had many difficult choices to make at seventeen years of age, and most were challenged. I chose to go to the police in order to help other women avoid my pain, but instead of being listened to, I was interrogated. Years later, I found out my rapist tried to assault another woman, something I live with daily. I share in chapter 3 how working on self-worth and self-love helped me let go of guilt and regret for not being able to do more.

I was judged for bringing a child into this world under horrific circumstances, yet no one could understand the love and energy I felt inside of me. And really, why did it matter when it was my body and the repercussions were mine to deal with? At times I got tired of the judgment and stopped sharing my thoughts.

Long before my son was born, I knew I'd not only birth him but raise him. I never told anyone, not even my family. My parents and I agreed to hold off this discussion until after the birth. However, I found out quickly that by not asserting myself and speaking up, others would try to make choices for me. Imagine my surprise when a nurse told me that my social services counselor, the one I was assured I could trust, arranged for my child to be sent to foster care without my consent.

My counselor was on vacation when I gave birth. This was a gift from God. I can't imagine the judgment and negative energy that would have been brought into the hospital room if she had been there. The betrayal I felt from a woman I trusted added insult to injury, and I was left to face the mess she caused with her dishonesty. I asked for the phone and called the foster mom on behalf of my newborn baby. "I'm sorry, but no one told me about these plans. I decided to take my son home." She was sweet and kind on the other end: "I'm happy for you. Good luck, and just know that if you change your mind, there's a crib here waiting for him." I felt relief for not being judged.

I waited to call my counselor until she returned from vacation. Mom offered, but I wanted to regain the power that had been stripped from me. I sat on my parents' bed and nervously said the words through the phone, "I decided to keep my son." She replied, "You are making the biggest mistake of your life. I had this set up for you. How are you going to go to college and make a life for yourself? You are giving up everything." Ah yes. The words of judgment from someone who would have made a different choice. These words, believe it or not, meant everything to me. I vowed to prove her wrong.

I honor my resilient younger self for standing in her courage, faith, and love when she could have given up on the world over and over again. My parents and I made a pact: I could live at home and raise my son as long as I enrolled at University of Wisconsin-Madison and graduated. "Perfect, because that was my plan," I said, determined to create a better life for us both.

My family became my source of strength and light. While I felt the world was failing me, one person continued to remind me that I could walk through this and become stronger as a result:

my mom. I turned to her for words of support, affirmation, and guidance through this harrowing mess. I felt abandoned by many in my tight-knit town, though I prefer to believe it was never intended.

Why didn't the police—or others—do more? It's a question I have come to terms with. The answer is: my truth wasn't believed by authorities, and so others didn't believe me either. This never, ever should have happened. Through my struggles with isolation, Mom encouraged me to walk down Main Street beside her, holding both our heads high so others could see I did no wrong. I learned a valuable lesson at a tender age: *the first person who needs to believe in you is* you. This experience, as hard as it was, became the birthplace of my book.

By the age of twenty-one, I had fallen deeply in love with the man who would become my husband. I knew the first night we met. Funny, smart, charismatic, loving, kind, handsome, and so good with my son. We married on July 22, 1995. I graduated that same year with a degree in art education, we moved to St. Louis, Missouri, and I started my teaching career in the fall. My dreams were coming true.

Over the years we had two more boys together and moved several times, eventually residing in our dream home just four blocks away from the beach in sunny California. I soon gave up teaching to raise our sons, support my husband's career, and volunteer my spare time in the community. Yes, I was *that mom* who put together community-wide kickball tournaments, coached her sons' winning basketball teams, organized holiday block parties (painting Merry Christmas on the road with what I thought was washable paint!), and hosted sushi parties for water polo parents with way too much sake. I *loved* my life.

And then at the age of forty, my second round of trauma began when I found out my husband, David, had been leading a double life for most of our seventeen-year marriage.

Discovery was Thanksgiving Eve 2013. That morning, before he left for work, he'd hugged me at the front door—my last hug from the man I once knew. I will always remember that moment. "I promise to be home early so we can prepare for tomorrow," he said.

I was looking forward to prepping for forty-six guests, but as the night dragged on and David never showed, I grew frantic and worried. When he finally arrived at our front door after 10:00 p.m., he was hallucinating on drugs. I was blindsided.

Over the following five days, I held myself together and celebrated Thanksgiving as planned, while my worst nightmare unfolded. Disclosure of the details he'd been hiding were horrifying. My husband was denying his truth that he was gay, while acting out on his own secret struggles, betraying me with men while also abusing drugs, alcohol, and sex.

I remember the jolt of reality when I realized our marriage was obliterated. Complex posttraumatic stress disorder (PTSD) froze my body, while emotions of rage, sadness, and loss overwhelmed me. *Do I run or do I stay? What do I do? Someone tell me what to do!* I was thrown back into the trauma from when I was seventeen years old. *Who can I trust?* In fight-or-flight, I yearned to feel protected in my husband's arms, while simultaneously wanting nothing to do with the monster who had destroyed our family.

I spent this year trying to understand and make sense of how this had happened. A happy family who had it all, and suddenly I had nothing—and no one knew this but me. I was the only person on earth who could understand the firestorm of emotions I was living in, yet I was the only person who could get us through this chaos. So I continued to dive into my husband's past, looking through a life he was leading behind my back. I wanted to know, how did he get to this place? I searched phone calls, messages, and chats with men on platforms I never knew existed. Most betrayed partners wouldn't want to see it all, but I demanded every detail to be shown so I could process and move through this debilitating time. What I quickly realized was that his dark, double life was even deeper than I could have imagined. Mutual friends knew about his addictions, lies, and deceit, but not one person told me about his struggles. A mom on my son's basketball team I coached was dealing my husband drugs in our back alley. Mutual friends also became his lovers, while remaining friends with us both. Facts after facts after facts were brought to light, and all I could think about were our sons. *How do I protect my boys?* As trauma brain set in, many times I wondered if I'd even make it through.

Nature Heals

It was during this time that I found what saved my life: *nature*. Nearly every day I grabbed my stand-up paddleboard and set out four miles offshore on the Pacific Ocean, to let go of my pain and somatically heal. The ocean became a refuge while dolphins and whales became my best friends. Dolphins are known to be protective, playful creatures, reminding us to approach life with a sense of joy and humor while staying in tune with our instincts.[1] Whales, on the other hand, are known for their compassion and solitude. They understand the journey of both life and death, reminding us to stay creative while here on this earth.² Most days they would find me, sometimes rolling over while looking me in the eye as if to say, "I see you. It's gonna be okay." It's no wonder they showed up often during a period of my life that was so uncertain.

When not on the water, I hit the trails, running or hiking. As a child and adult, I always loved the outdoors. I once even took my two youngest kids on a six-week road trip to nine national parks. However, prior to this traumatic experience, I'd never used nature for intentional healing purposes. For five consecutive years, I ran fifty-mile ultramarathons on Catalina Island, California. Goals were big for me; I needed something to strive for. Every time I achieved something new, I believed in my ability to overcome my trauma. I set out to summit peaks in Southern California, Yosemite, and the Grand Canyon. When standing on a mountain or in the canyon, I could assess how small, yet connected, I am in this world, and how much of an impact one person can make. Many of these climbs happened while my kids were in school, or over a few days when my oldest son or their father (post rehab) took over. The greatest beauty in my adventures was sharing what I learned with my children. We lead through example.

The wild became my life source, my home away from home, and where I felt most spiritually connected—as it is in many cultures. In "Indigenous Americans: Spirituality and Ecos," Jack D. Forbes wrote, "Most or perhaps all Native Americans see the entire universe as being alive—that is, as having movement and an ability to act. But more than that, indigenous Americans tend to see this living world as a fantastic and beautiful creation engendering extremely powerful feelings of gratitude and indebtedness, obliging us to behave as if we are related to one another."[3] Nature provides messages and answers we seek in life—all we are asked to do is listen.

Various native cultures use the terms *spirit animal, animal guide*, or *spirit helper* to "describe spirits of benevolent nature, usually helping someone during a hard time. These spirits can bring strength, insight, and even a sense or feeling to someone who needs it."[4] Many times birds would swoop low overhead when I needed a message of compassion and support. I asked my deceased grandparents for a sign of hope, to tell me it would be okay, and a monarch butterfly landed in my hand, where it played for over ten minutes. As Black Elk, the well-known Lakota medicine man, wrote, "All of nature is in us, all of us is in nature."[5]

The more I connected with nature, the more I connected with my body, mind, and spirit—and found the clarity I needed to move forward. This was my biggest year of growth and where I learned the depth of my ability to heal and forgive.

When I was forty-one, my husband moved out, and at forty-two, I started my business when I felt a calling to share my story and teach through my experiences. *Was I the only one going through this? How could I be?* A part of my soul was drawn to create something far bigger than the world had experienced before. Sure, my story needed to be heard so others didn't feel alone. At the same time, victims needed an opportunity to heal in a way that wasn't yet being offered. I knew nature was the vessel because I experienced the healing it provided. Floating on my paddleboard a few miles offshore with a friend, I shared my idea to create Transformational Grand Canyon Retreats. His answer was, "Oh my God. Please, Sara, do it." And so I did.

Many have asked me, "Why the Grand Canyon?" I've learned through my own trauma recovery that we must go deep within ourselves and sit with who we are, in order to climb out of our pain and transform. Metaphorically, the canyon works—and it's one of the most spiritually connected spaces I've hiked in.

At forty-three, I made the decision to sell our 4,200-square-foot dream home and 95 percent of our belongings. Most items made their way onto Nextdoor or Facebook in exchange for two of my favorite things in 2017: wine and lemons (the latter for my hot water, honey-lemon drink). I told Dan, my real-estate agent/therapist/confidant wrapped in one, to find the *perfect* family of five to buy our home and pick up where I left off, renovating it how I hoped. I also wanted it sold by Memorial Day, and I promised him it would happen. So I envisioned this lucky family in my home: a happy couple, three kids, and a dog. I prayed for and manifested on this family while, one by one, I let go of memories our family of five had created in that space. And right before Memorial Day, the family of five I envisioned bought our home and immediately began renovations. During that same time, my boys and I moved directly across the street into an 850-square-foot rental unit and Marie Kondo'd our space, only bringing in items that had meaning and touched our souls. *Explain that to ten- and fifteen-year-old boys!* I was determined for my kids to learn all they could from this process of unraveling and rebuilding. Also, I no longer felt financially and physically strapped to a house, and instead I was freed up to focus on my business. I felt confident we'd be more than okay.

At forty-four, my divorce was final, my business was picking up, and I agreed to be the subject of a documentary, *Walk Through This: A Story of Starting Over*. At forty-five, I finished my book proposal and set out on the High Sierra Trail with three women for eight days in August, playing in the mountains from Sequoia National Park to the summit of Mount Whitney, while manifesting a literary agent. Hiking trails and fishing in lakes, I asked the universe to "please guide me to my literary agent by December 31, 2018"—something no one thought possible, but my intuition said otherwise. And then I received the sign. One day when I was eating lunch at Precipice Lake with the only female solo hiker we encountered on the trail, she pulled a book of poetry from her pack. "I'm working through personal trauma on the trail and this book has helped me." I looked at my niece and said, "My book will be carried on the trail some-day too." Wouldn't you know it? I was offered representation by Folio Literary Management in New York City the morning of December 31, 2018.

Now, at forty-six, I'm happier than I have ever been in my personal, family, and business life. I've stood on a TEDx Manhattan Beach Talk stage and spoken about forgiving; filmed the documentary in the Grand Canyon; guided women and men on transformational, healing retreats; met amazing people on my journey; and brought my book to fruition. I smashed through many hard, frustrating, and scary barriers to get here. And as many people do, sometimes I wondered, *Why me? What did I do in my past life to deserve this bullsh*t?* It's funny how my internal conversation always ended with, *Why not?* I was raised to believe that we are all created equal and never to lead with ego. So I learned to accept when life became hard and to work through my pain as best I knew how. When depression, anger, or sadness set in, my mind would float back to the message handed to me at eighteen: *Someday you will write a book and give others hope so they don't feel alone. Stay courageous and strong.* Because of those words, I began to believe that *life was happening for me, not against me.* What I do have control over is believing in and manifesting my positive life into existence, while learning from the struggles I am handed. We all have this ability! So here I am, typing words I knew twenty-eight years ago would someday be written. Little did I know the content that God or the universe would be creating through me. How can I not feel honored, blessed, and grateful?

Your Heart and Soul Picked You

I was guiding a group of women in the Grand Canyon, and we were deep in discussion. A woman from the group was beating herself up in conversation when I stated, "Your heart picked you. Please be kind and gentle with yourself." Those words stopped us on the trail and began a self-reflection of love. (Thank you, spirit, for working through me and sharing the words we needed to hear.) We can be our biggest critic and judge ourselves so harshly. Or we can place our hands over this beautiful heart that was created for us and love who we are in the moment, not passing judgment for how we feel or think, and simply accepting that we are doing the best we can right now. Your heart and soul picked you. Be kind to you.

This powerful moment on the trail began an internal conversation. *If I'm nothing more than a human being walking this earth, how have I worked so quickly through my traumas? Why do I love myself so deeply when others feel so much sadness, pain, limited self-worth, and little self-love?* My realization was quite simple yet profound.

What has saved me all these years is the intimate relationship I have developed with my heart, soul, and emotions. That's it—nothing more. The most important relationship you have is the one within yourself. It is often said that we are handed a lesson over and over until the lesson is learned. I believe my old soul has a lot of wisdom to share, while also having many, *many* lessons to learn. That said, I also know that I'm here for a short time on earth and let's face it, there's a lot to explore. Perhaps it's driven by my stubbornness (my oldest son mentioned I have a bit in me), but I would rather dance with joy than sit in my own sh*t. I learned quickly that no one was going to do the work for me or tell me the best way to heal from all that I have gone through in life. So I became my own teacher, and nature became my therapy. It was there I learned how to feel the feels, process emotions, connect even more deeply with my heart and soul, and move on to forgiveness, freedom, and peace.

Honor Your Journey

We have all lived through setbacks and some sort of trauma. We know this, yet I've witnessed people judge and compare their own life experiences against another's time and time again. Our internal narrative loops statements and words that we begin to believe. *Of course that would happen to me. They have more resources to get help. I have nothing. I have no one. What I went through is far worse. At least I'm not them.* We inevitably use self-judgment to hold us in a victim state, keeping us from seeing our traumas, feeling our emotions, and holding us from safety. Why? Because getting vulnerable with ourselves can get messy and uncomfortable. Yet we can never heal our deepest wounds if we refuse to acknowledge the emotions that lie under our masked pain.

When we separate ourselves from judgment, comparison, and attachment to others' experiences, we give ourselves freedom to heal and grow the way we feel works best for us. To give you an example, I've sat in many conversations with women who have been betrayed by their husbands, and vice versa. You may be shocked at how many people have said, "It was probably easier to move through your betrayal because he was with men and not women. At least you knew that it had nothing to do with you." But how would any of us know when we haven't walked in one another's shoes? My deepest healing began when I stopped comparing my experiences to others, judging my traumas, or attaching to the details of my story. These are experiences that have happened in our lives. They do not define us unless we let them.

In place of judgment, consider honoring your trauma and setbacks. Doing so changes your focus from *How could this happen?* to *How can I heal, learn, and grow?* Shift your energy from the victim state ever so slightly to a place of love and ask yourself, *How do I want to be outside of this pain?* I asked myself this question over and over again through my own healing process. Slowly, I peeled back the layers of who I am as a woman, partner, mom, friend, and so many other parts. Finding my personal values shed light on my purpose and how I chose to be outside of my painful past.

At the underlying core, here is what I found: *my willingness to forgive has continuously brought me back to love.* For example, I think back to the moment my husband disclosed his multiple affairs and double life the morning of November 29, 2013. Listening to him share lies and deceit was horrifying. Yet I knew enough to separate from his words and affirm us both. I told him, "What you did was wrong. I want a divorce. But I will forgive you someday." Perhaps it was my seventeen-year-old subconscious self speaking, knowing I had to get to this place of love to be free from the toxicity of emotions that would otherwise unravel within me.

Others noticed my transformation and began to ask questions. "How have you gotten to this place when you have been wronged so deeply? Why aren't you more angry?" What I found through these conversations was how much people judge forgiveness. They feel that to forgive those who hurt them most, they must forget the action that created the hurt. I didn't realize how much this was true until researching the topic of forgiveness for my TEDx Manhattan Beach Talk. *Why is this so hard to do?* Then I looked up the definition of forgiveness, and what I found astounded me.

Merriam-Webster defines *forgive* as:

> to cease to feel resentment against (an offender):
> pardon (e.g., *forgive* one's enemies)
> to grant forgiveness (e.g., had to
> learn to *forgive* and forget)[6]

We are taught that to forgive, we must forget and move on. Yet how can we honor our difficult experiences when forgetting they occurred? It's impossible. I am asking you to consider looking at forgiveness through an entirely different lens. One that allows you to honor what happened, while validating your emotions and experiences. It's not about condoning the actions of those who hurt you. It's about handing responsibility to your offender, no longer carrying the pain, and bringing in freedom and peace to replace the toxic emotions you've been holding on to.

I define *forgive* as:

> to acknowledge an offense and the
> consequences of that offense as truth,
> to choose to let go of negative feelings,
> and to cease to harbor animosity toward the offender

Many are afraid of granting forgiveness for fear of becoming weak. Victims find what they think is power in anger, judgment, accountability, and the ever-so-popular grudge. But when living daily in these toxic emotions, our energy is being placed where our offender no longer lives. Do they really care that you are feeling this way? Are they bothered that you're holding anger, judgment, or a grudge over them? Probably not, or they wouldn't have wronged you in the first place. Strength and power are not found in toxic emotions. They are found in the form of joy, happiness, and love.

This book walks you through my seven steps to healing, as I share my personal methods for embracing forgiveness. This process is meant for both men and women. Just like setbacks and trauma in life do not discriminate, healing is meant for everyone. I share how we are all ripples of change for one another in this world. We cannot leave anyone—regardless of age, race, religion, color, creed, gender, or sexual orientation—out of the discussion.

It's time to create a better world. Let's turn the page and begin.

Preface

Learning the Science of Trauma and Manifesting a Path to Healing

*D*uring my trauma recovery, many times I felt alone and not listened to. My reason for feeling this way was twofold: I was living in a nightmare no one understood, and I was healing from this nightmare in an unconventional way—from standing in awe on a mountain peak with tears rolling down my face, to having what I thought was a profound life conversation with a close friend and hearing her say, "I don't get it. What are you talking about?"

My healing through nature, meditation, and somatic trauma therapy was deep, uncovering layers of pain, past patterns, and feelings of negative self-worth, but also discovering so much hope. I changed because of this process. Transformed, really. I knew it and could feel it, and others could see and feel it too. Even my therapist and coach said, "I've never seen another recovery quite like yours."

I became curious. Why didn't I stay in PTSD mode, living with acute trauma brain and depression like so many others? What was different about me and the tools I was using to work through this versus others in my shoes? I'm an experiential learner and teacher. But what I uncovered through literary research fascinated me.

To support your healing journey, you must have a general understanding of

- what trauma and trauma brain are and how they affect your body,
- nature-deficit disorder and how nature healing works,
- our seven energy chakras, and
- how to use this book on your road to forgiveness.

This section is a precise and succinct discussion of scientific research, spiritual beliefs, and personal experiences. For those wanting to dive deeper into these concepts, refer to the resources list at the end of this book.

As a reminder, I am neither a doctor nor a therapist. However, I am a professional coach and certified through the Association for Partners of Sex Addicts Trauma Specialists (APSATS). My life has become a textbook, with firsthand knowledge and experience dealing with trauma, its effects, and how to heal.

What Trauma and Trauma Brain Are and How They Affect Your Body

According to the American Psychological Association, "Trauma is an emotional response to a terrible event like an accident, rape, or natural disaster. Immediately after the event, shock and denial are typical. Longer-term reactions include unpredictable emotions, flashbacks, strained relationships, and even physical symptoms like headaches or nausea. While these feelings are normal, some people have difficulty moving on with their lives."[1]

Trauma is more common than many people realize, and it can happen to anyone. According to the National Center for PTSD, approximately 60 percent of men and 50 percent of women experience at least one trauma in their lives.[2] Women are more likely to experience some form of sexual harassment, child sexual abuse, and/or assault in their lifetime; men are more likely to experience accidents, physical assault, combat, disaster, or witness death or injury.

If the stress of a trauma (or traumas) reaches clinical levels, it can be diagnosed as posttraumatic stress disorder, or PTSD. This is often "characterized by episodes of reexperiencing the trauma, avoidance of situations that are reminiscent of the trauma, emotional numbing, and increased arousal."[3] In the United States approximately 7 to 8 percent of the population will experience PTSD sometime in their lives. Further, eight million adults have PTSD during a given year (and that number is a low estimate), and about 10 percent of women and 4 percent of men develop PTSD at some point in their lives.[4]

As I'm writing this, we're experiencing a global pandemic with COVID-19. Many doctors, nurses, health-care workers, patients, and family members will emerge from this ordeal with lasting posttraumatic symptoms.[5] Can you imagine having one respirator, two patients, and having to decide who lives? Or watching people die with fear in their eyes and no family present? And these same family members aren't able to grieve or memorialize appropriately.[6] Many are being asked to stay safe at home, yet they share homes with abusive husbands, wives, partners, or parents. And those dealing with depression, anxiety, or addictions have no meetings to attend, therapists to see, or facilities to utilize, and providers are trying virtual care to bridge the gap.[7]

We're living in an unprecedented time. Therefore it's crucial, like never before, to understand and destigmatize the effects of trauma. Let's continue with learning more about trauma so we can "shed the shame" and promote healing.

Trauma is experienced in one of two ways.[8] *Direct trauma* impacts a person directly, by physically experiencing or witnessing the event unfold. For example, children raised in a home with domestic violence may exhibit trauma symptoms as a result of hearing or seeing the abuse. *Indirect trauma*, otherwise known as "secondary trauma," impacts a person differently. The person doesn't physically experience the traumatic event or witness it unfold. Instead, traumatic events are learned about through secondary accounts. Symptoms of both include anxiety, stress, depression, insomnia, and flashbacks.

There are three main types of trauma: acute, chronic, and complex.[9]

Acute trauma results from a single incident, such as a car accident, theft, or natural disaster. The incident doesn't happen over a prolonged period of time.

Chronic trauma is repeated and prolonged, such as abuse or domestic violence. Chronic trauma also can have a layering effect. You may have a time in your life when you experience multiple traumatic events at once, such as a disease and a car accident, your marriage falling apart and losing your career. One doesn't protect you from the other. Rather, you may find yourself feeling more intense posttraumatic stress or symptoms as a result.

Complex trauma "refers to traumatic stressors that are interpersonal, that is, they are premeditated, planned, and caused by other humans, such as violating and/or exploitation of another person."[10] These events are oftentimes planned, extreme, and/or ongoing. In complex trauma, a partner may feel trapped and develop various coping mechanisms—such as alcohol and drug use, eating disorders, or self-harm—and can also suffer from low self-esteem and identity issues. When bonds have been deeply interwoven because of commitments, child-rearing, living together, and shared experiences (whether good or bad), it can feel impossible for a partner to free themselves from a toxic, abusive relationship.[11]

I should know. It took me nine months to gain strength and leave because of complex trauma and *trauma bonding*, a term developed by Dr. Patrick Carnes. Trauma bonding occurs when a narcissistic partner uses "fear, excitement, sexual feelings, and sexual physiology to entangle another person."[12] Past trauma can lead to trauma bonding as well, and because I hadn't addressed issues from my rape at seventeen, it makes sense how I was led down this destructive path. Being in a relationship with my husband, I didn't have to examine my underlying issues with self-esteem, self-worth, sex, and intimacy after my body and psyche had been violated. I gravitated toward a partner who courted and doted on me and made me feel like I was all he ever wanted. The deeper our bond grew, the more codependent I became. And when our relationship began to erode due to his manipulations, hidden addictions, and deceptions, I felt shame, responsibility, and blame. I tried anything and everything to be good enough and fix what was broken, not realizing that I could never be what he was looking for because of his unprofessed sexuality.

The more I reached out for love or recognition from my husband, the more our trauma bond was strengthened. All he had to do was *love bomb* me—inundate me with love and devotion to maintain trust and attraction—and the toxic cycle of abuse and responsibility continued.[13] The focus stayed on him, us, and the kids, and it stayed off me and his double life.

Many people who experience complex trauma may have difficulty establishing safe and healthy relationships later on. For example, children who experienced or witnessed abuse in their homes will normalize the behavior and become numb to, or have issues with, healthy intimacy.[14] If we only know a home that is unsafe, it makes sense that we would be drawn to the same later in life. Is it possible to experience a healthy relationship? Yes. But it's necessary to acknowledge any generational patterns, take responsibility, work on your traumas, and relearn what a healthy intimate relationship is.

Understanding Relational Trauma and Betrayal Trauma

Over twenty-one million women will experience relational and/or betrayal trauma in their partnership.[15] Infidelity is considered one of the most emotionally traumatic and stressful events a person can go through.[16] Dr. Barbara Steffens, my colleague and leading partner-trauma specialist, stated, "Relational trauma, often called attachment injuries, occurs when one person betrays, abandons, or refuses to provide support for another person with whom he or she has developed an attachment bond."[17] Because this occurs within the context of an intimate relationship, the emotional responses to betrayal and infidelity mirror that of other traumatic events, creating anxiety, shock, depression, and posttraumatic symptoms.

Betrayal trauma is trauma inflicted by someone a person is close to and reliant upon for support and survival.[18] Betrayals can appear as broken trust or promises, lies, deceit, sexual affairs, or affairs of the heart. My spouse, unbeknownst to me, struggled with drug, alcohol, and sex addiction. Uncovering years of betrayal by searching his phone, internet activity, and chats was horrifying. It was also a reason why I became certified to work with partner trauma in the field of sex and pornography addiction.

In his book *Out of the Shadows: Understanding Sexual Addiction*, Dr. Patrick Carnes likens sex addiction to drug and alcohol dependency: "The addict's relationship with a mood-altering experience becomes central to his life."[19] Another colleague of mine, Elizabeth Poth, a specialist in the fields of sexual addiction and partner betrayal trauma, shared this insight:

> When I concurrently worked at my private practice, as well as at the largest emergency room in Wisconsin, I witnessed time and again the astounding similarities between individuals who struggle with drug and alcohol dependency and sexual addiction. . . . I concluded that the basic hallmarks of alcohol, drug, and sexual addiction are: dependency, frequency, duration, and consequences. One of the many consequences the sex addict must face is the partner's betrayal trauma

experience. The person she loves and thought she was safe with has a secret sexual life. Now what? Hence, the search to understand, "What is sex addiction?"[20]

Before my relational and betrayal trauma six years ago, I had never heard of sex addiction. The surge of technology—our access to pornography and online platforms and sites, as well as our ability to "hide behind screens" while leading double lives— has created new waves of trauma for partners around the globe.

So how does relational and betrayal trauma happen?

We're taught that trust, respect, and shared goals are the foundation for a healthy relationship. We allow ourselves to be vulnerable, let our guard down, and trust unconditionally, expecting others to do the same. Our devoted friends and family members wouldn't hurt us, right?

But then it happens. And when it does, oftentimes the betrayed partner will exhibit posttraumatic symptoms ranging from hypervigilance, ruminating thoughts, rage, anxiety, and depression. Feelings of helplessness can become so overwhelming you doubt you'll ever recover. I not only uncovered relational and betrayal trauma within my marriage, but I discovered multiple blows of betrayal trauma involving friendships and institutions. In some instances, the posttraumatic stress symptoms were heightened because my children were indirectly involved. Because of this, two betrayals by friends were more difficult to forgive than those with my husband.

It's important to understand and acknowledge all the traumas you are facing in order to heal from them. In this book, I share the process I used to forgive every person who betrayed me.

Understanding Trauma Brain and
How Trauma Affects Your Body

Trauma brain was an important concept for me to understand in recovery, primarily because I felt like I was losing my mind. In the first year, I tried to make sense of my life and the betrayals. It was like living in a fog bank, unsure of which direction I was headed. Some days I had it all together and felt like Superwoman—and other days I felt lost and defeated, with ruminating thoughts of despair.

My husband would get annoyed with my questions: "How did this happen?" "When were you doing this again?" "But why, and weren't you ashamed?" "Tell me again—who were you with?" While I sought answers, his impatience grew. Unlike me, he was provided the help he needed through an inpatient treatment center in Malibu, California. No one knew or understood what I was going through, so he became the person I turned to for validation of my fears and feelings. That was unfair to him—and me—because he was also my trigger. My colleague, Dr. Janice Caudill, defines trauma triggers as "anything that serves as a reminder of painful events in your life. They can be people, places, things, or situations."[21]

Later in my professional career, I was able to sit down with a now-colleague, who was affiliated with the treatment center at the time, and share how it felt to have my husband cared for while I was left to go home to three kids, alone, without direction and feeling ashamed and helpless. It's fair to say I experienced a form of treatment-induced trauma, even though I wasn't the one being treated. When I did go in for counseling sessions at the center, I was labeled as a "coaddict" in my husband's sex, drug, and alcohol addictions. *How could I be a coaddict when I didn't even know it was happening?* I thought.

Finally, when I met my therapist and partner-betrayal trauma specialist, Dorit Reichental, I learned I was experiencing relational and betrayal trauma, not coaddiction, and I wasn't going crazy. She explained that my mind wasn't working as it used to because of trauma brain. Dorit and Dan Drake, a certified sex addiction therapist, were instrumental in my growth and healing during this portion of my recovery, and I am forever grateful to have them in my personal and professional life. If you aren't finding the help you seek, please reach out through my website for guidance (https://www .saraschultingkranz.com). No one should go through what I did—everyone deserves to receive compassionate, professional treatment for recovery.

Let's break down the brain and learn what happens when experiencing trauma brain. In the 1960s, American neuroscientist Paul MacLean formulated the "triune brain" model, based on research indicating that the brain develops from the bottom up and is divided into three distinct regions.[22] In his book *The Body Keeps the Score*, Dr. Bessel van der Kolk follows this model to distinguish how trauma affects the brain and body:

- *The brainstem or primitive brain*, responsible for the most basic survival mechanisms, such as sleep/wake, hunger/ satiation, body temperature, and breathing. Threats to survival are first passed through the primitive brain.
- *The limbic brain or emotional brain*, which holds the hippocampus, amygdala, and hypothalamus. The limbic brain is responsible for initiating the fight-or-flight response to

keep us safe. Because of this, trauma can have a major impact on its functioning throughout life.

- *The prefrontal cortex or executive brain*, responsible for high-order conscious activity, language, abstract thought, imagination, and creativity. The prefrontal cortex develops last, is affected by trauma exposure, and is vulnerable to going offline in response to threat.[23]

In addition to being labeled a coaddict during the first several months of my recovery, I was also assumed to be codependent. At times in my relationship that was the case. But it's important to recognize that when victims are triggered and experiencing PTSD, "what's often labeled codependency is the brain seeking safety while trying to make sense of reality."[24] Triggers often don't make sense to the outside world. For example, every man I encountered who fit a certain profile became my husband's possible affair partner.

One evening, a few months after my husband was released from rehab, we attended his stepsister's wedding at a beautiful country club in Los Angeles. You wouldn't have known by looking at me in a skintight black gown and stilettos that inside I was fragile, broken, and raw. Every moment was spent trying to make sense of the last seventeen years with the man beside me.

Sitting at dinner, a young, handsome waiter leaned over and served our meals. Perhaps it was the glance between my husband and this stranger, or the way my husband said, "Thank you." My body froze while my mind questioned, *Oh my God, have they slept together?* I wanted to run. I wanted to be held. I wanted to cry, scream, know the truth, and protect my babies back home.

That evening before bed, I asked him, "Did you sleep with

the waiter? I know this sounds crazy. But he fits the profile you are attracted to. Did you?"

He looked at me, shocked, and said, "You've got to be kidding me. No. I didn't. When is this going to stop?" I rolled over and cried myself to sleep.

It was emotionally exhausting and mentally draining to be in a constant state of chaos. But my brain wouldn't stop.

Although I didn't understand what was happening at the time, my experience was common for someone in my situation. According to the article "Betrayal Trauma Addiction," "When triggered, the right brain's amygdala, which is in charge of processing emotional responses, makes a very quick decision to begin the fight-or-flight response. This is a physiological reaction that happens when there's a perceived danger. The amygdala's danger signals trigger the release of stress hormones such as adrenaline and cortisol. This increases one's heart rate, blood pressure, and breathing, preparing us to fight or run."[25]

Let's use the encounter with the waiter as an example. When his presence triggered me, my amygdala began firing and I wanted to both freeze and run. PTSD effects flooded my body. Meanwhile, my left hippocampus was trying to make sense of my memories, present moment, timeline, and life story: *What is true and what is false? Could he have slept with this man? He fits the profile, but why would my husband even want to sleep with men? What in my marriage was true? Who have I been all of these years to my husband? And if I am no longer his wife, who am I?*

My brain was trying to create safety in the present while using memories from the past. But how can that be accomplished when new information doesn't align with old memories? Continual flashbacks and reliving memories can, in many ways, hold us in the past and be more harmful than the trauma itself. I asked the same question hundreds of times, over and over, "Did you sleep with him?" The answer didn't matter—neither did the fact that I was seeking answers from a man who'd lied to me for nearly seventeen years. In the early part of recovery, I was grabbing at straws to make sense of my life. Victims can't help it.

How did this trauma affect my brain differently than when I was raped at seventeen? Details were stored differently by my trauma at forty than they were at seventeen. As mentioned in the introduction, I have incomplete memories of what happened that night. I can hear my rapist's voice and disturbing laughter in my mind, and I remember *Saturday Night Live* in the background, even as I type this. But I don't recall specifics of what happened, which is common for trauma survivors. As Dr. James Hopper and Dr. David Lisak wrote, victims "will remember some aspects of the experience in exquisitely painful detail" and "remember other aspects not at all, or only in jumbled and confused fragments."[26]

It is not possible—nor should it be expected—for trauma survivors to remember details they can't even recall from their happiest days. Not to mention that memories are stored differently during those events. One of the most challenging and difficult aspects of living through trauma is knowing something happened, yet being questioned, judged, and shamed for not remembering all that unfolded. My hope is by understanding the brain and what happens during trauma, we can find better ways to support victims through the criminal justice system and on their healing journeys.

Trauma from my husband's discovery affected my body and nervous system in scary ways. I lost my appetite yet forced myself to eat an apple a day. I barely slept, and I often found myself dissociating from the present moment. One time I was running with my friend Sue, and I hit a light pole. Did I see it? Yes. But I couldn't judge it correctly with my brain "offline." My shoulder battered and bleeding, I both laughed and cried. And I still have the scar to remind me.

As van der Kolk stated, "After trauma the world is experienced with a different nervous system. The survivor's energy now becomes focused on suppressing inner chaos, at the expense of spontaneous involvement in their life. These attempts to maintain control over unbearable physiological reactions can result in a whole range of physical symptoms, including fibromyalgia, chronic fatigue, and other autoimmune diseases. This explains why it is critical for trauma treatment to engage the entire organism, body, mind, and brain."[27]

So how do we progress? Van der Kolk stated, "The challenge of trauma treatment is not only dealing with the past but, even more, enhancing the quality of day-to-day experience. One reason that traumatic memories become dominant in PTSD is that it's so difficult to feel truly alive right now. When you can't be fully here, you go to the places where you did feel alive—even if those places are filled with horror and misery."[28] In other words, when living with trauma and PTSD, we crave normalcy. If we cannot find aliveness in the moment, we resort to our past, where we once felt what it was to live. The problem is, those memories are now tainted. As survivors, we must reclaim our lives and create new memories of being alive to replace the traumatic memories. We must find even the smallest joy and pleasure in the now.

This is where my trauma healing became fun, and where it becomes enjoyable for my clients today. Once I began reclaiming my life by exploring nature and finding joy, my brain and mind began to shift. Stepping out of your comfort zone to see the world from a new perspective fosters insight into your life. Every time I climbed another peak, spent time outdoors, or paddled on the ocean with dolphins and whales, I felt a rebirth.

Like van der Kolk, I don't believe in desensitizing clients from their past traumas. In fact, I encourage them to process the experience that has led them here today, feel their emotions, bring their brain and body back "online," and when ready, release themselves from the entanglement of their past by forgiving those who hurt them. My passion is guiding clients—traumatized and not—to live fully in the present. As van der Kolk wrote, "If you cannot feel satisfaction in ordinary everyday things like taking a walk, cooking a meal, or playing with your kids, life will pass you by."[29]

Nature-Deficit Disorder and How Nature Healing Works

Richard Louv, author of the bestsellers *Last Child in the Woods* and *The Nature Principle*, coined the phrase "nature-deficit disorder" to explain how our societal disconnect with nature and the outdoors impacts our health. Louv stated that "nature-deficit disorder is not a clinically recognized condition, but rather a description of the human costs of alienation from nature." Nature-deficit disorder affects "health, spiritual well-being, and many other areas, including [people's] ability to feel ultimately alive." Symptoms include attention problems, obesity, anxiety, depression, fear of the natural world, and disregard for life.[30]

Society is pulling itself from the very place—nature—where we "feel ultimately alive," according to Louv.[31] Yet, according to van der Kolk, what we need most in trauma treatment is to "feel truly alive right now," while living "fully and securely in the present."[32] Immersing myself in nature, while also accessing somatic trauma therapy—talk therapy combined with "mind-body exercises and other physical techniques to help release the pent-up tension that is negatively affecting your physical and emotional wellbeing"[33]—was key to moving my healing forward. Being in the wild awakens us, and we can access these moments from our memory whenever necessary. By teaching ourselves to feel into our bodies while redirecting our thoughts, we retrain and rewire neural pathways in the brain to ultimately feel peace and gratitude in the moment.

For example, during recovery, when I felt down or hopeless, I closed my eyes, sat in silence, and noticed the sensations in my body. Whereas I once went to a place of asking, *Why did he do this to me?* and *How did this happen?* I began to guide my thoughts to a moment in nature when I felt inspired and energized. When in trauma, I'd experienced a lump in my throat, tightness in my chest, and a sinking feeling in my stomach. When alive in nature, I felt courageous and strong from my gut, heart, and mind. These times became reminders that I do have control over my response to events in my life, despite what I previously believed. And now I encourage my clients in this same way.

However, it's difficult to bring up a moment in nature when you're rarely, if ever, outdoors. According to the Environmental Protection Agency, the average American spends 87 percent of their life indoors and another 6 percent in automobiles. Only 7 percent of our entire life is spent outdoors.[34] And while we're indoors, adults spend about eleven hours a day staring at some kind of screen, whether a computer, phone, tablet, TV, or another type of electronic device.[35] On average, US teens spend more than seven hours per day on screen media for entertainment, and tweens spend nearly five hours—and that doesn't include time spent using screens for school and homework.[36] We are distancing ourselves from our natural world by spending most of our time in man-made environments.

With adults spending so much time indoors, it's no surprise that children are doing the same. "Kids can grow up fine without nature," said Louv, "but with it, there are marked improvements in attention deficit hyperactivity disorder, learning ability, creativity, and mental, psychological and spiritual health. When you consider that in some US schools, up to 30% of boys are now on Ritalin. . . . I've lost count of the number of teachers and youth leaders who have told me how different kids become when you get them out into nature. Trouble-makers become leaders. Nature is their Ritalin."[37]

It's hard to ignore the mental health crisis we're facing in this world. In 2018, according to Statista, 4.21 billion prescriptions were administered in the United States, compared to 3.95 billion in 2009.[38] One in ten people struggles with substance use, including addiction to prescription drugs.[39] In 2016, more than forty-six people died every day from overdoses involving prescription opioids.[40] In 2017, nearly thirty-eight thousand persons of working age (sixteen to sixty-four years) in the United States died by suicide, which represents a 40 percent rate increase in less than two decades.[41] Our society is struggling. Yet I believe there's hope.

The World Health Organization defines health as "a state of complete physical, mental, and social well-being and not merely the absence of disease or infirmity," with the belief that "the enjoyment of the highest attainable standard of health is one of the fundamental rights of every human being without distinction of race, religion, political belief, economic or social condition."[42] A recent study in *The International Journal of Environmental Science and Technology* found that getting outside for as little as five minutes per day improves both mood and self-esteem.[43] And Florence Williams, author of the bestselling book *The Nature Fix: Why Nature Makes Us Happier, Healthier, and More Creative*, wrote that our "epidemic dislocation from the outdoors" is destructive to our mental and physical health. The therapy is straightforward: "The more nature, the better you feel" and "engaging with nature or wildlife can reduce trauma symptoms."[44]

At the time I discovered my husband's betrayal, my boys were twenty-two, twelve, and seven years old—three distinct ages. I worried about their needs and futures. Directing attention on each child, while also dealing with my husband's addictions, required a lot of mental, physical, and emotional energy. Days filled staring at computer screens, running errands, crying in a tub, configuring schedules, picking kids up from school, or driving between sports practices were unsustainable. I felt depleted and exhausted.

When I read Williams's book, I understood why:

Stanford neuroscientist Daniel Levitin points out in *The Organized Mind*, our brain's processing speed is surprisingly slow, about 120 bits per second. For perspective, it takes 60 bits per second just to understand one person speaking to us. Directed attention, or voluntary attention, is a limited resource. When it flags, we make mistakes; we get irritable. Moreover, task-switching, which is something we do an awful lot of these days, burns up precious oxygenated glucose from the prefrontal cortex and other areas of the brain, and this is energy we need for both cognitive and physical performance. It's no wonder it feels pretty good to space out and watch a butterfly. . . . In a real biological sense, we have more things to keep track of than our brains were designed to handle.[45]

How does nature affect the brain? Williams shared research from David Strayer, a cognitive psychologist at the University of Utah's Applied Cognition Lab:

The way Strayer sees it, moving through any environment engages three main networks in the brain. There's the executive network, which includes the intellectual, task-focused prefrontal cortex and does most of that stimulus and behavioral inhibition. There's the spatial network, which orients us and does what it sounds like. Then there's the default network, which kicks in when the executive network flags. They are yin and yang, oil and water, working only in opposition. You can only engage one or the other at any point in time. . . . When people are overly ruminative, depressed, self-involved, and self-critical, the default network is blamed by psychologists. Yet it is also credited with producing empathy, creativity, and height of insight.[46]

Williams wrote, "One of the compelling theories about nature is that it acts like an advanced drug, a sort of smart pill that works selectively on the default network in the way new estrogen therapy makes bones stronger by targeting some estrogen receptors in the body but not others that might increase cancer risk. It would appear that when we have a positive nature experience, it engages what's good in the default network without allowing us to wallow too much in what's problematic."[47]

Every time I hiked a trail, stood on a peak, noticed rainbows in the sky, observed butterflies, watched a spider weave a web, or looked into the eye of a whale, my imagination and creativity would flow. Those moments would draw on many regions across my brain, including the hippocampus, "where memories are formed and stored, and the medial prefrontal cortex, which is involved in self-focused processing, including autobiographical memories and planning."[48] Earlier, we talked about van der Kolk's belief that in trauma treatment we need to "create new memories in the present" where we "feel truly alive right now." Accessing the default network "enables us to imagine other perspectives and scenarios, envision the future, remember the past, understand ourselves and others, and create meaning from our experiences."[49] "'You let the prefrontal cortex rest, and all of a sudden these flashes of insight come to you,' Strayer says. 'It supports creativity, positive well-being, reductions in stress. There are all kinds of reasons why it's helpful.'"[50]

Additionally, Williams wrote, "Beginning in the early 1980s, Stephen and Rachel Kaplan at the University of Michigan, noticed that psychological distress was often related to mental fatigue" and that "our constant daily treadmill of tasks was wearing out our frontal lobes."[51] The Kaplans' findings made sense to me, someone whose brain sometimes felt "tired." Life didn't stop because I experienced trauma. I had a house to manage, schedules to maintain, and kids to juggle—and my body was drained from sadness and rage. Williams asked Rachel Kaplan the same question I had: If we know what leads to mental fatigue, what allows the brain to rest?

"Soft fascination," was Kaplan's reply.[52]

Neuroscientists believe that "soft fascination" is the best

condition to initiate the default network. This state occurs when watching a sunset, listening to rain, or observing a bird on a tree branch. Your attention is gently focused on what's happening around you, unlike during "hard fascination," when you're deeply focused on the stimuli overwhelming your senses, such as a siren or a scream.[53]

"Soft fascination" became my new favorite term. I'd tell myself, *Find five minutes a day of soft fascination in nature—for you.*

I remember the day I read *The Nature Fix*. I was walking my dog and reading while highlighting sentence after sentence. To dive into the nature-brain connection was an awakening. I'd been using nature to heal all along without even knowing it. You'll hear me speak a lot about self-care and taking care of you. You can't underestimate the importance of these types of activities. Give your ruminating mind a rest, awaken your heart, and enliven your body in nature. Take a short walk. Step outside and breathe. Grab a nap under a tree. Listen to the birds. You will thank yourself for giving yourself permission to experience even brief moments of soft fascination.

Our Seven Energy Chakras

Science has shown that everything in our universe is composed of energy.[54] Humans and animals are all made of pure energy, and we share it with the earth, which gives and sustains life. I touch on this throughout the book as it relates to the earth; human emotional, mental, and physical states; as well as the energy that we give and receive, such as love and forgiveness. Through my practice of nature healing, forgiveness, and meditation, I found it helpful to learn the seven chakras—often referenced when practicing yoga, meditation, or breathwork—and better understand human energy from a spiritual space. If this information is new to you, please remain open to what I am about to share.

Chakra is an old Sanskrit word that means "wheel." Your life force—otherwise known as *prana energy*—is rotating inside of you. "This spinning energy has seven centers in your body, starting at the base of your spine and moving all the way up to the top of your head."[55] When all seven chakras are open, energy runs through you freely, and you feel balanced in body, mind, and spirit. Let's take a closer look at each chakra.[56]

The Root Chakra or *Muladhara*

Located at the base of your spine, the root chakra provides you with a sense of being grounded. When we feel like we can stand on our own two feet and take on challenges, our root chakra is clear and open. When it's blocked, we feel unsteady, as when we're in fight-or-flight mode. The most important thing we can do when feeling trauma symptoms or threatened is to find safety by grounding ourselves to the earth. We discuss our root chakra in step two, when finding our inner warrior—the strength and heartbeat of who we are.

The Sacral Chakra or *Svadhisthana*

Your sacral chakra is located at the pelvis (or lower abdomen) and helps you regulate your emotions and desires. This is home to your creative life force energy and sexual energy, guiding you to enjoy life while here on Earth. Your sacral chakra is associated with the water element—adaptability, creativity, inspiration, fluidity, and emotions. It's no wonder so much of my healing and inspiration for life was found while stand-up paddleboarding on the ocean.

The Solar Plexus or *Manipura*

Have you ever felt butterflies or had a sinking feeling in your stomach? That was your solar plexus at work. It's here that we find our confidence, self-worth, and personal power, and where we're able to navigate our lives using our wisdom and core values. We learn more about and uncover our personal power/inner warrior and core values in step two. From our solar plexus, we can process and let go of what doesn't serve us, ultimately allowing us to live in peace and freedom.

The Heart Chakra or *Anahata*

The heart chakra is located at the heart center. It's associated with emotional qualities, such as compassion, joy, inner peace, empathy, and openness. Your heart chakra is the bridge between the lower chakras and the upper chakras, and influences your ability to give and receive love. My fierce sense of hope for my life and future has always radiated from my heart chakra.

The Throat Chakra or *Vishuddha*

The throat chakra rests right above the heart and gives voice to your personal truths. This is where you find your authenticity and vulnerability for self-expression and your own inner power. We can speak honestly, with clarity, compassion, and love for self and others—sharing how we truly feel—without apprehension. Speaking the truth about my trauma and past experiences was crucial to finding forgiveness.

The Third-Eye Chakra or *Ajna*

The third-eye is located between your eyebrows and holds conscious and unconscious awareness. It's here that we find our heightened intuition, imagination—for example, when our default brain is turned "on"—our inner knowing, and extra-sensory perception. I lead my life open to information from beyond the material world. From this space, we learn deeply about ourselves: mentally, spiritually, and emotionally.

The Crown Chakra or *Sahasrara*

The crown chakra sits at the crown of your head and is said to be "the doorway into pure consciousness."[57] We're able to fully connect spiritually with the universe through consciousness energy. And we're able to function from our highest self, in a more enlightened way, with both inner and outer beauty.

Human beings are constantly seeking ways to balance prana energy within their lives—whether it's through yoga, meditation, walking, other movement, or stillness. In fact, we aren't alone. All of life is always shifting and finding harmony in this world. I draw upon nature, plants, and animals for education, inspiration, metaphors, and analogies. I'd like to share a passage from *The Hidden Life of Trees*, by bestselling author Peter Wohlleben. I was in awe reading this paragraph because of how much I could relate to a chapter called "The Sick Tree":

> Statistically speaking, most species of trees can live to a ripe old age. In the burial area of the forest I manage, tree buy-ers always ask how long their tree might live. Mostly, they

choose beeches or oaks, and as far as we know, these trees usually live to be between four hundred and five hundred years old. But what is a statistic worth when you apply it to an individual tree? Just as much as it is worth when you apply it to an individual person—nothing. The anticipated trajectory of a tree's life can change at any time for any number of reasons. Its health depends on the stability of the forest ecosystem. It's better if temperature, moisture, and light conditions don't change abruptly, because trees react extremely slowly. But even when all the external conditions are optimal, insects, fungi, bacteria, and viruses are always lurking, waiting for the chance to strike. That usually happens only when a tree gets out of balance. Under normal circumstances, a tree carefully apportions its energy. The largest portion is used for daily living: the tree has to breathe, "digest" its food, supply its fungal allies with sugar, and grow a bit every day. Then the tree has to keep hidden reserves of energy on hand to fight off pests.[58]

To harness the healing power of nature, we must believe that as with trees, "the anticipated trajectory of [our] life can change at any time for any number of reasons." If you find yourself in a place where your world is unstable, it's time to *get back into balance* and *carefully apportion your energy.*

From your root chakra, ground yourself in the sand, grass, or dirt, and feel support from Mother Earth. Sense the energy of the flowers, trees, animals, and wind. When using this book, begin to take note of what you're feeling on your skin, such as the cold air, warm sun, and brisk breeze. Pay attention to your own energy when outdoors versus when indoors. Are you happier in fresh air? A great way to note what's happening within you is by asking yourself, *Where am I feeling this in my body?* Your body speaks—all you need to do is listen.

How to Use This Book on Your Road to Forgiveness

The power of mindset is huge in the self-help community. Though I find this concept necessary and helpful, you cannot *mindset* your way through forgiveness. You can certainly try. But you will always land back where you began.

To heal anything, you have to feel everything. You must walk through your experiences and your pains, and you have to embrace everything around you that got you to where you are at this moment. Every piece of us must be explored like a new trail, every rock uncovered where we find new treasures about ourselves. We must be honest about our past, find moments of inspiration that keep our lives magical, and access hope to carry us through stormy days and dark nights.

Life is meant to be felt and lived.

That is why I bring together body, mind, soul, spirit, and nature in this book. Though I was raised Catholic and have struggled with how I've been treated within my religion, I do believe in God. I also believe in the spirit of the universe. I have felt spirits within the Grand Canyon, on mountain peaks, and on my personal hiking journeys. I have felt nature's spiritual energy as I have locked eyes with whales, turtles, dolphins, and insects. And I've witnessed mystical and unexplainable weather patterns that have left me knowing there is something way bigger than any of us in this universe. In my writing, you'll hear me use the terms *spirit*, *universe*, and *God*. As you read this book and do the work, please access and use whatever higher power feels right for you. And when I speak of "soul" in my writing, I refer to the animate life or deep-seated passions and desires that comprise who we are.

Seven steps are presented in this book. Steps one through six are meant to deepen your personal understanding, responsibility for, worthiness of, and love for self. Step seven is devoted to the process of forgiving. At the beginning of every step, you'll find what's covered in the chapter. If what I share doesn't speak to you in the moment, perhaps it will at a later date. We all require different tools in our trauma recovery journey at various times.

Get creative when using this book. You can take notes in the margins or even doodle nature drawings throughout, if this helps you process and absorb the content. If possible, I encourage you to do all meditating and journal writing while sitting outdoors with your journal, pen, and favorite drink. You can lean against a tree or simply be on your back deck. Breathing in the fresh air will slow your mind and provide nature's healing qualities. If you need to stay indoors, push your chair next to a window (open it if you can), where you are connected visually to nature. And if you are immobile, you can invite nature into your experience by listening to nature sounds on your phone or other device. Both viewing nature and listening to natural sounds have proven to support healing and have positive mental health benefits.[59]

Within this book, I'll be guiding you through several meditations and visualizations in nature. There is no right or wrong way to do these. Also, you can download audio versions of all med-

itations and visualizations from my website (saraschultingkranz
.com/walkthroughthisresources.com).

A friend once said to me, "I didn't realize until recently that
all along, I was climbing mountains wrong. I put my head down
and rushed to the summit. I spent a few moments on a peak, took
a picture, and then I ran back down. But now sitting here with
you, listening to all of the things you've explored in life, what do
I have to show? Just a time stamp saying I beat my old record. I
missed the journey. And I won't do that again."

So congratulations, my friend. This is your journey. And
yes, it will be hard, messy, and perhaps even confusing and
uncomfortable at times. But all I ask of you is to show up and do
the work. Let it unfold as it is meant to, because it will.

If you hear me talk about concepts that are new to you, that's
okay. As I mentioned, I've provided a list of resources at the end
of the book. You can also access my website for more information, or find me on social media and ask your burning questions.
We need community at this time, which is why I've created community through my site and in the work I do. And I'd love to be
brought on your forgiveness journey! Share your personal findings, stories, realizations, and "aha" moments in nature. Let's all
be sources of truth, inspiration, and hope for one another.

Set Your Intention and Surrender

*Y*ou have to pick one. Would you want to know *how* you die? Or *when* you die?" my twenty-one-year-old niece, Grace, asked me recently as the two of us were hiking down a mountain.

"You are kidding, right? What kind of a question is that?" I replied. We were hurrying to the car before dark, climbing over rocks and through snow, the last people on the trail. Grace wouldn't let up, and I could feel my annoyance building. I love philosophy and deep conversations. But her question felt ridiculous.

Stopping, I asked, "What would you choose?"

"I think it's a stupid question too. But if I had to choose? I'd choose when. And then I'd do everything I love without fear, all out."

I laughed at the irony of her words. Two women, standing on the side of a mountain they'd just summited in snow, with the night settling in.

"Grace, hon—you are doing that already."

Between our birth and our death, our story and unknowns lie. I know my purpose, and I know why I do what I do in life. But I won't know all of the reasons I'm here until my last breath is taken. When I leave this earth, will I have written and published more books? I hope so. Maybe I'll have stood on stage with my favorite mentors, sharing our truth, while inspiring the crowd and extending hope into the world. Or perhaps I'll have adventured around the globe and finally explored every place I've wanted to see. As a reformed perfectionist, my life has taught me to release the grip and allow life to unfold.

Remember, there are beautiful nuggets of learning in everything. In step one, I encourage you to do the following:

- Show up doing this work with a childlike sense within you. Play, explore, sit in awe, and have fun. Laughter has always been a healing tool for me, and I would like it to be that for you too.

- Take the pressure off yourself when making choices. Many choices and decisions must be made in any trauma recovery or healing journey. And because we may have trauma brain (read more about this in the preface), I realize this can be hard to do, which is why I placed this in step one. I share my three-step practice to bring clarity into your decision-making process. I'd love for you to implement this in your life.

- Set your intention and surrender. I share why intentions are important and how to set them. I'll guide you through a meditation to find your intention for this journey.
- Have peace moments, which are felt when we sit in nature and feel present. I share the five-step process I use to awaken my senses and experience these moments.

When I was twelve years old, I began looking at life through a different lens.

It was a snowy evening in December 1985. Alone, walking the empty streets of my village, I stopped under a streetlight at the bottom of a hill. Looking up to the dark sky, I watched as majestic snowflakes drifted to the earth. The world fell silent and still as an overwhelming calm and peaceful sensation swept over me. I thought, *I feel alone right now. As if everything has stopped. What's going on? What is this feeling?*

This experience wasn't something I talked about. To be honest, I couldn't even put words to that moment. But through the years, I longed for more of what I felt that night. So I continued paying attention to the little things that enlightened me and brought back that feeling. I found myself watching clouds overhead, staring at blades of grass, and noticing how birds have intricately detailed feathers. After I began personal development and spiritual work, I identified that what I felt long ago—and now seek in my daily life—is a state of *awe*.

A Childlike Sense

As children, most of us released pressure to be perfect and instead live in a perpetual cycle of learning, growth, bewilderment, and awe. Exploration and trying new things are a part of growing up. We are taught that to become better at anything, failure along the way is expected and, in many cases, encouraged. As a former art teacher, I fostered my students' creativity and encouraged them to create without judgment. "Art," I'd say, "like living, is an experience. Don't be afraid to get messy and have fun."

I like to think of us as having iterations—or versions of who we are—within ourselves. These parts, including who we were as creative children, build upon one another to form the people we are today. So if this is the case, why can't we access our inner child, who climbed trees and viewed life with wonder? Or the little girl who twirled in her first dress? When going through hard times in life, why can't we speak to our twelve-year-old self, who stood under the streetlight and felt awe while viewing something as simple as snowflakes falling from the night sky?

We can, and it's important to do so. In fact, "awe—as opposed to joy, pride, amusement, contentment, and other positive emotions—is the singular sensation that goes the furthest in boosting one's overall sense of well-being."[1] It's no wonder that so many new clients say to me, "I want to be happy again, like I was as a child. I want simplicity back in my life." When accessing the part of us that explores life, we become active participants in our lives rather than spectators. Being an active participant will guide you to places you never thought possible—standing on a mountain, freeing yourself from the entanglement of past relationships, becoming CEO of a company you love, or finding forgiveness from your deepest pain. When doing the work in this book, I encourage you to call on the child within you and release unneeded pressures. We must not be afraid to get messy and have fun.

Let me share an example from my experience.

Take the Pressure Off of Choices

It was Labor Day weekend 2019. I was hiking the High Sierra Loop in Yosemite National Park for seven days with Grace and a dear friend, Cocco. At one point on the trail, Cocco chose to finish her journey early and hike out, while Grace and I trekked on to complete what we set out to do. On night six we snuggled in our sleeping bags on a large bed of rock beside a tranquil waterfall. The sky was full of twinkling lights and shooting stars.

Waking early, we boiled water for coffee and oatmeal while looking at the map and sharing our thoughts for our hardest day yet. Eventually the trail would come to a fork where a decision had to be made. We could take a less scenic, easier route, or push through and hike the more difficult yet beautiful option. Over the years I've learned the importance of having a plan while always giving yourself the option to pivot at any time. In this case, we folded the map, set out on the trail, and chose not to decide until we needed to.

After hiking through a mile or so of tall pine trees, we arrived at the fork. Grace asked, "So, which way should we go?"

My body was already tired and sore. In many ways, it would have been preferable to pick the easy trail. But before answering my niece, I took a breath and listened to my heart. The childlike adventurer within me was speaking loud and clear. I responded,

"If we leave not experiencing the one we came to view, how would we feel?"

Laughing, she replied, "Yeah, I knew we'd be taking the harder one. We came to experience the trail. I would be sad if we missed out on the view."

Wherever you are in your life journey, decisions must be made. Perhaps you are at a crossroads and feeling pressure to decide if you should leave your marriage, start a new career, or move across the country. I hear you. I wrote this book because the choices in my own life brought me to where I am today. Some provided lessons. Others brought celebrations.

In step two, you'll learn how to embrace your inner warrior and make choices aligned with your values. But first, it's important to create a healthy foundation for life and within our decision-making processes, one that encourages you to "be good to you." I've learned a valuable lesson on my journey: do not put undue pressure on yourself when making choices in life. This is especially important for trauma survivors. I encourage you to read that lesson again. And listen to your heart—be good to you.

We self-inflict pressure to make the "right choices." But when we don't have a clear understanding of what choice to make, we question our abilities and self-worth, only creating more barriers to our answers. *What if I don't do it correctly? What if I fail? How will people judge my decision? I'm too old. I'm too young.* Inevitably, the loop of criticism and questioning holds us in a place of stagnation, unwilling and unable to move forward. We become frozen in our own procrastination, sometimes blaming others for our inability to decide, and we project our anxiety into the world.

We often force decision making. It's the "get it done" attitude. According to researchers at Cornell University, we make

226.7 decisions each day on just food alone![2] Imagine how many choices we make daily or in our lifetime. Our frontal lobe is set into overdrive from thinking, depleting us and leading us to make irrational, spur-of-the-moment choices based on fear or exhaustion. When a decision is made from this space, we're more apt to question or feel self-doubt. How many times have we shamed ourselves after the fact for making what we suddenly "feel" is the wrong choice? Even with all of my personal development and spiritual work over the years, it's easy to get caught up in the shame-game when feeling the repercussions of making the wrong choice. So I've learned not to make decisions when in a state of fear or exhaustion, or when I don't feel aligned in a mental, spiritual, emotional, and physical space. Opting out of societal and self-inflicted pressure, while being in relationship with my values and inner warrior, has freed my ability to find answers quickly and without second-guessing.

I'm not suggesting that we flow through life making choices and then not hold ourselves and others responsible for the successes or failures of those choices. And I'm certainly not saying, "Flip a coin to decide the most important decisions in your life." Yes, your choices matter. But when you make a resonant choice after gathering your facts, thoughts, and emotions, let that choice be what it is—a choice.

By releasing pressure when making a choice, we

- replace anxiety with peace;
- open ourselves to learning and possibilities;
- welcome clarity to our mind, heart, spirit, and soul; and
- step into a decision with commitment from our highest self.

Clarity is needed to make any decision in life. As a business-woman and single mom to three sons, I make thousands of choices and solve many problems daily. Even simple choices, like what to have for dinner, can feel overwhelming after a long day. When struggling to make a choice, I daily release pressure and invite clarity into my decision-making process using a three-part practice.

Part 1: Leave the Chaos

Step out of your physical environment. The space surrounding us holds our ability—and struggle—to make choices. For example, I find it extremely difficult to make a peaceful decision when my kids are being raucous around me. To gain clarity, you have to shift the energy around you. I invite you to go outdoors, even if the weather is cold and wet. Most of my creativity, clarity, and awe-filled moments have been in rain, snow, and freezing weather. If possible, take off your shoes and put your feet on the earth. Close your eyes and take a few deep breaths. Slow your mind and settle into your body. You are not being asked to do anything at this moment but breathe. Don't worry if your mind wanders. Take note of what comes forward.

Part 2: Ask Your Higher Self for Guidance

The answers to all of your questions are already within your heart and soul. When I share this with clients, they sometimes get upset with me. And rightfully so. We are taught to search outwardly for answers. If we don't know something, we ask our mom, dad, siblings, therapist, coach, friends, or smart device for the answer. Although they can provide you with facts, they can't give you an answer. Any of these people or devices can tell you what to do based on what they know, but unless the answer comes from within you, it's not your answer—it's theirs. I know, hearing that can sting!

While fact gathering is an essential tool, we must also access our higher self for guidance, opening our heightened intuition and inner knowing from our third-eye chakra, which we learned about in the preface. I invite you to do so through this simple meditation. Stand grounded with your feet on the earth, place both hands over your heart, close your eyes, breathe deep, and slowly say these words:

> *My dearest [insert your name],*
> *Show me the way. Please lead me with love as you guide*
> *me to the answers I seek. I trust you. I love you. I am listening.*

Continue these words until you feel a shift within your body. Your mind, breath, and thoughts will slow. Answers may begin to unfold without hesitation. Other times we need to surrender and allow the decision-making process to do its job. This is a powerful meditation that will guide you on your journey.

Part 3: Ask for Signs

Through trauma recovery, I have learned that we are all spiritually connected and have the ability to ask for guidance and clarity, if it be from nature or God. Around 2004, I went through a very difficult period, when my husband was faced with a health scare that threatened to prevent us from having more children. I'd always envisioned being a mom to three or four kids.

The situation presented more questions than answers, and I lived in a constant state of fear and anxiety. Once again, I looked to the sky for peace and awe. I've always believed in angels, even as a little girl, and at one point I asked them to show me the way. Not long after, a song by the group Train, "Calling All Angels," played every time I turned on the radio. Once, I found it so ridiculous that I changed the station three times to test my angels. Every station had that song playing at the same time. Talk about a message! My angels provided guidance, strength, support, clarity, and love through the lyrics:

> I need a sign to let me know you're here . . .
> I won't give up if you don't give up[3]

All I needed to do was listen and trust that I was supported through my pain.

During that time, I also began seeing the number 444 repeatedly. I didn't ask to see the numbers. They just kept appearing: on my clock, on passing vehicle license plates, on receipts from the store—I even received a random check in the mail for $444.84. I couldn't make sense of it, so I spoke to my friends about what was happening. Kelly and I cochaired the school district's art department; spirituality and angels were a part of her life. "None of this is crazy," she said. "In fact, it makes perfect sense. Listen, and research what it means."

I went to Barnes & Noble and purchased my first book about angel numbers. What I found astounded me. According to past spiritual guides and today's bestselling author Kyle Gray, who wrote *Angel Number: The Message and Meaning behind 11:11 and Other Number Sequences*, 444 is a message from your guardian angels that you are protected, supported, safe, and loved. Your angels surround you and remind you that you don't have to do everything on your own.[4] Even today, I repeatedly see the numbers 444.

At other points in my life, I have felt most connected with

those who have passed before me. For the past six years, I have asked for signs and clarity from my grandparents. They are usually provided by way of nature, numbers, and scents. My grandpa Schulting passed away in 1998 and is generally the first to communicate. Perhaps this is because I was alone at his bedside in the middle of the night and during the final hours of his life, asking him to stay with me while our family gathered for his death. We developed a powerful connection in that short time. He was also a lover of water and nature. For the first year of my trauma recovery, I would stand-up paddleboard and talk to him while on the open ocean. Not surprisingly, dolphins and whales would emerge. These visits gave me clarity, hope, and strength.

I always ask for signs from spirits, ancestors, and nature, and when guiding clients or on my personal trips in the mountains and canyons. Whether the Navajo, Hopi, or other tribes, I feel their spirits and ask for protection, love, support, and guidance in my decision-making process while on the trail. I ask for these signs by way of animals, weather patterns, or other means. I trust their spirits are with us every step of our journey. Throughout this book, I share unexplainable and powerful spiritual experiences we have had in nature.

In this third part of the practice, let's invite clarity into your decision-making process by requesting signs. Keep it simple. With your feet grounded to the earth, eyes closed, and your hands over your heart, take a deep breath in and request:

[Insert universe, God, nature, spirit, those who have passed, or your angels],

   Please provide me with signs and clarity through my decision-making process and while on my life journey.

If you would like to get specific with your request, please do so. But when you ask for a specific sign, remember it may not show up in a living form. You may notice your signs in the most random places. So pay attention, remain open to receiving, and begin noticing patterns in numbers, animals that cross your path, and signs in nature. For example, I always see heart-shaped rocks while hiking, and I do so when I'm speaking or thinking of someone I care about. I encourage you to start a journal and take note of

- what new signs you're noticing,
- when these signs are crossing your path, and
- what thoughts are going through your mind when your signs are provided to you.

Bring this process into your daily practice and witness how your decision-making shifts when you release pressure to make choices in life, and instead trust that you are being guided on your road to healing, growth, and forgiveness.

Set Your Intention and Surrender

An *intention* is a statement that supports who we want to be and how we choose to show up in our lives. Different than goal setting, daily intentions allow us to live in the present moment, ultimately guiding us toward our highest good. An intention may be, "I am living my day with fierce self-compassion as I am worthy, I am loved, and I matter" or "I intend to write from truth, inspiration, and hope, to create peace and freedom in readers' lives." Without having a clear understanding of why we are doing anything in life, we are steered from our true calling. That said, we don't want to stay attached to the outcome of our intention. When we try to control the outcome, we get in the way of allowing things to happen when or how they are meant to.

Let's go back to when Grace and I were at the fork on the trail. That was a great example of how our intention—not pressure to make the right choice—became a guide in our decision-making process. When we set out on the trail, our intention was to hike the Lewis Creek route and climb over Vogelsang Pass at nearly 10,700 feet, where we hoped for a heightened state of awe. The Lewis Creek route is slightly longer and gains 800 feet more elevation before descending into camp. It is a steady uphill climb gaining over 3,000 feet in six miles. I was already in so much pain and knew heading this route would probably break me into tears, which it did. Before making the decision on which route to take, I dropped into my heart and looked at our choices as well as our potential consequences, something I've been teaching Grace to do. The easier route seemed like the sensible way to go. However, my heart pulled me to seek the destination my soul longed for. I reminded myself that pain is temporary, but memories are lifelong.

And thankfully, we followed our souls' calling. Many times climbing up the pass I questioned our decision from a mind-set space. When the questions snuck in, I knew my brain was focused on the pain and not the journey. Some moments, taking one more step seemed like one too many. When this happened, I stopped on the trail and looked at the vastness below me. The beauty was breathtaking! In fact, sitting at my computer, I'm transported back to the trail and tears are welling in my eyes.

The most accomplished writer cannot describe the feeling. Everywhere you turn, there are majestic mountains, clear lakes, and streams fed by waterfalls flowing with such energy. Little purple flowers were blooming, bugs were playing, and birds were swooping down from overhead. The air was peaceful.

Climbing just over the pass, we met four hikers who stopped and said, "Drop your packs just below Vogelsang Peak and rock scramble to the top for an even better view." I believe that we cross paths with others for a reason, whether it's to express an idea, share a message, or provide direction. Grace knew this about me and said, "Sara, what's another eight hundred feet in elevation, right? He told us to do this for a reason!" When I thought I was finished hiking for the day, I found myself scrambling rocks on the side of another mountain that I didn't know was possible to summit. At times I wondered, *What am I doing here?* Forty-five minutes later, I knew why. Taking my last step onto the peak, I looked out in awe and wept in wonder. When led by intentions and the adventurous spirit we once embraced as children, we open ourselves to possibilities and experiences far more meaningful and greater than we ever thought possible.

Intention setting has kept me on a path of self-discovery, healing, and growth, and has led me to forgiveness. Your intentions will do the same for you. Creating daily intentions shifts attention from the big picture—your long-standing yearly or life goals—to the steps taken in order to get there.

In my life today, I set goals every January for the new year. For a period of three years before and during the discovery of my husband's betrayal, I stopped creating yearly goals because they felt too overwhelming (though I did create short-term goals). For the purposes of this book, I focus on intention setting because I found it significantly more useful in my healing process. Setting intentions connected me to the present moment and became a guide to open and align with my higher consciousness, or crown chakra. This practice also has become a driving force to connect spiritually with the universe and nature, while manifesting and fulfilling my long-standing goals. By setting intentions, I discovered freedom, clarity, love, strength, and so many other qualities.

You can set intentions for most anything. Below are a few ways I utilized them during trauma recovery and use them still in my daily life. I set intentions:

- for my day (example: *I intend to live in gratitude today.*);
- before every hike, paddleboard, run, or walk (example: *I intend to stay present in nature and invite calm, peace, and joy while being guided by my ancestors.*);
- if I'm feeling an unpleasant emotion regarding a situation, a person, or an experience (example: *I intend to release my [insert emotion] for [insert situation or person] and invite love, peace, and harmony.*).

Intention setting is important because we can't make resonant, life-changing steps without having a clear understanding of what we're hoping to find. Setting daily intentions will awaken your mind, heart, spirit, soul, and body to what is possible. Every intention you place has energy and purpose. You cannot set an intention from negativity and doubt, and you cannot force your intention. You must fully believe in your intention and its value, and be willing to receive as your intention comes to fruition. When setting your intention, remember the following:

Keep Your Intention Honest

Creating intention is a practice of being honest with yourself. What is it that you seek? Why are you here? What emotion or thought do you want to release? What are you ready to welcome in? These are a few questions I ask all of my clients.

If you're holding on to anger toward a particular person or situation, examine whether you're ready and willing to release these emotions in order to bring in love, joy, and peace. Honesty with yourself begins here. Do you even *want* to face those emotions and release the toxicity? Many times we say we want to let go of anger, but we have been conditioned to hold power in this emotion. I've had clients say to me, "I want to forgive, but I'm scared to let go of my anger. The anger reminds me that what he [or she] did is wrong." Being honest means looking at your life and saying, "Yes, I am ready and willing." When you say yes, your way of thinking and your perspective begin to shift. For example, by releasing the anger toward the offender, you are inviting love, freedom, and power to yourself. Creating false intentions, or ones you aren't aligned with, will only create frustration when you don't receive what you seek.

Allow Your Intention to Evolve

When we attempt to control the process, we miss the magic of life along the way. And likewise, when we attach to an outcome we hope to receive, we limit the possibilities of what could happen. I explain to clients that the intention they hold going into the Grand Canyon may not be one that's in store for them. As an example, I had a client, Michelle M., who went into the canyon with the intention of sorting through her personal life. Michelle was continuously provided signs, while on the trail and in group conversations, that to create joy in life, she needed to leave her career path, something she hadn't even considered. Hanging out at the beach next to the Colorado River after a long day of hiking, I said, "You're going to quit your job." I saw the clarity in Michelle's words and actions before she saw it herself. She replied, "No, I'm not!" Shrugging my shoulders, I said, "Okay."

The next day we stopped on the trail to talk with another hiker. He said, "The best thing I ever did was leave my burn-out corporate career in finance. That life was ruining me." I looked at Michelle and smiled as she stood there, shocked. It was validation for what was possible.

Michelle did quit her job, and she's never been happier. "Getting away from all of the noise and settling into who I am, rather than who I was trying to be, sparked me to quit. It had been a long time since I'd felt comfortable in my own skin and since I had done something for myself, so once I did, I wasn't sure why I was living any other way."[5] We must stop controlling and instead watch and listen.

Keep Your Intention Positive

Use words that have a positive impact and healthy energy attached. I love the phrase "What you feed, grows." If you create intentions with negative words, your energy will not be aligned to create positive results. For instance, instead of saying, "My intention is to fight my anger," you could say, "My intention is to invite love, harmony, and freedom into my life, releasing the toxicity of anger." Do you notice and feel the shift from the first example to the second?

Feel into Your Intention

"Feel the feels" is something I say a lot. For your intentions to have results, you must align your beliefs with the outcome you hope for, and feel into your intention and journey. If tears surface, give yourself permission to cry. If laughter bubbles up, let it out. Scream if you feel called to do so. Emotions are simply energy in motion. It's counterproductive to bottle up what is ready to be released.

Brittany Lynne is one of my coleads on retreats, and she'd recently separated from her husband. As usually happens, whether you're guiding or not, I expected her to move through suppressed emotions—especially since this was the same place I had gone through that process after the loss of my marriage. Standing on Plateau Point, where it felt safe, I encouraged her to release her feelings into the canyon by screaming over the rim. Anger, sadness, rage, and loss—let it all go. It's not always easy to release our emotions, especially when we've been taught to "hold it together." But it's crucial to remember: *to heal anything, we must feel everything.*

Now that we have spent time understanding intention setting, I will lead you through a short guided meditation that is focused on setting your intention.

Guided Meditation for Setting Intentions

Let's begin by grounding ourselves to Mother Earth.
Sink your body into the earth or place your feet on the
     ground.
Close your eyes and place both hands over your heart.

Take a deep breath in and hold it.

Mother Earth is holding and supporting you throughout this journey.

Release your breath.

Take another deep breath in and hold it at the top of your inhale.

Imagine that breath coming from the deepest place within you.

And now release the breath.

Like a bird flying in the sky, allow your thoughts to wander and be free.

There is no right or wrong to this meditation.

Now envision yourself standing on a mountain with the vastness and beauty below you. There are majestic trees as far as your eyes can see. The air is fresh. Your surroundings are serene.

Nothing else matters but this moment.

Take another deep breath in through your nose.

Imagine looking deep into the ravines and canyons below, allowing the breath to surface from the valley floor.

You are supported by spirit, nature, the universe, God, and angels.

Release the breath, exhaling through your mouth.

Let go of all inhibitions, judgments, shame, and criticism.

Imagine the wind lightly brushing your face. The sun gently touching your skin. You feel the earth below your feet.

Everything that surrounds you in this moment in nature is love.

Take another breath in through your nose, drawing in love, support, and peace from around you.

Sink into calm and release your breath out.

As you stand on this mountain, notice the beauty that exists below you.

Take a deep breath in through your nose.

Exhale again through your mouth and release anything that doesn't serve you.

Surrender to stillness.

Allow your mind to let go.

You are right where you need to be.

Now ask yourself, *What is my intention for this journey?*

Inhale through your nose.

Exhale through your mouth. And listen to your heart.

There's no need to judge what is being brought to light.

Simply be honest with yourself.

Feel into what you need.

Breathe in. And breathe out.

And again, ask yourself, *What is my intention for this journey that I'm on?*

Sink deeper into Mother Earth, and know you are supported, loved, and surrounded by peace.

Breathe in. And breathe out.

Be present with your feelings that arise.

If you feel a desire to cry, let yourself cry.

Sit in peace with what is coming through.

Again, there is no right or wrong to what surfaces.

What is my intention for this journey?

Feel into your intention.

Breathe in. And breathe out.

And when you are ready, begin to come back to this time and place.

Wiggle your fingers and toes.

Open your eyes and notice what is around you.

Take your intention with you as you move back into
 your day.

When you're ready, open your journal and complete this
sentence:

My intention for this journey is _____.

Continue writing about your experience. How did
this meditation make you feel? What emotions did you
experience? What did you see when standing on the
mountain? Free write—or write whatever comes to mind
without judgment of grammar, spelling, or content—in
your journal for as long as you need to. Bring forth all
that was brought up during this meditation.

Now that you have set an intention for this journey, pay
attention to what shifts in your life. Notice how you wake in the
morning or feel during the day. And pay attention to how people
respond. Take notes in your journal and look for patterns.

Also, remember that your intention may evolve, much like
Michelle's did. If that happens, you may decide to return to this
meditation and modify your intention statement.

Surrender to Peace Moments

Prior to their canyon experience, few clients of mine have
experienced what I like to call "peace moments." However,

peace moments are necessary for healing and growth. A peace moment occurs when you quiet your mind, settle into your heart, and are completely aligned with body, mind, spirit, nature, and the present moment. It feels as if everything around you, including time, has stopped. The energy around you shifts into stillness.

I'm going to share a five-part process that I use in nature daily, whether on a trail, on the beach, or sitting in the park. Take your time and do not rush through this. I encourage you, throughout this journey, to access this process whenever you feel called to do so. Please have your journal and pen close by.

- *Lie on the earth—don't be afraid to get dirty!* Dig your feet into the soil. Sit on a rock next to a creek or riverbed. Or lean up against a tree.
- *Close your eyes and take a few deep breaths.*
- *Notice what is happening within you as your mind, body, soul, and spirit connect with nature.* Let your mind slow and your shoulders drop while your body sinks into the earth. Don't force anything—just sit in peace.
- *Open your eyes and look around you at this moment. Pick up a piece of nature.* Maybe it's a pine cone, a rock, or a flower. Much of the information we receive about the outside world comes through our sensory organs: the eyes, ears, nose, tongue, and skin. Our nervous system processes this information to react, communicate, and keep the body healthy and safe. Go even deeper by connecting with nature through your five senses.
    —*Sight:* Take a look at the piece of nature in your hand. Pay attention to the color, details, patterns,

and shape. It's pretty amazing how we see an object differently when we focus on it.

— *Sound:* Hold your object to your ear. Does it make any sound when you touch it or move it around?

— *Smell:* Carefully hold your piece of nature to your nose, close your eyes, and inhale. What does it smell like? Inhale a second time and notice if the scent changes.

— *Taste:* Do not taste your object unless you know it is edible. If you're able to taste your object, please do so.

— *Touch:* Now touch what is in your hand. How does it feel? Try touching parts of the object and notice where its texture feels different.

Pull out your journal and write about your experience. How did it feel to lie on the earth and breathe in nature? What changed when your senses were focused on nature? Journal what happened within your mind, body, soul, and spirit.

When life gets unbearable or if the work within these chapters becomes overwhelming, come back to this exercise and ground yourself with the earth. Creating these peace moments will calm your mind and body.

Remember that every journey is different. Know that right now, you are where you are meant to be. I honor you for showing up! Step one on this path is an important one—please take it seriously and do the exercises. If needed, reread the chapter and go through the guided meditation any time.

In step two, we'll explore who you are in this world and who you would like to become. I love this chapter as we identify your values and connect with your inner warrior! The exercises within step two were the most powerful—and created the most shift—within my own trauma recovery journey. I look forward to guiding you.

Ask, "Who Am I?"

I was honored to be invited to present a TEDx Manhattan Beach Talk about my experience and the ways I'm helping people along their healing journeys. I brainstormed different topics with Kate, the curator and executive producer. Should I talk about nature therapy? How to step out of your comfort zone? Overcoming betrayal?

Our world today is infiltrated with gun violence, death, inequalities, and the effects of natural disasters. We watched in horror as fires engulfed Australia, possibly more than 480 million helpless animals dying in the devastation.[1] The United States is polarized by political parties and leaders spewing negative jargon through airwaves and social media. Narcissism and entitlement overshadow hard work when adults feel it's okay to buy their children's ways into universities.[2] With an inability to love and forgive without judgment, we lose our values and morals along the way, creating more chaos than peace. In turn, we've built a society of angry, lost, and confused human beings who have forgotten what it's like to live with kindness, truth, and inner happiness. It's quite sad. But it doesn't have to be this way.

Kate asked me, "How have you been through so much, and yet you're still okay?" I often get asked this question, at times with skepticism. I responded, "As crazy as it sounds, I work on forgiveness and taking responsibility for whatever part I play in everything that happens in my life." That piqued her interest, and she asked, "How do you define forgiveness?" I replied, "I hand back the pain caused by those who hurt me. It's about no longer holding what doesn't serve you, and allowing freedom, peace, and love to enter your heart."

This sparked a deep conversation about society's difficulty with forgiving. Is it our attachment to anger, fear, and resentment that causes the "what you did is unforgivable" narrative in our heads? Or do victims want perpetrators to see their pain in hopes their victimizers will feel shame, remorse, and guilt? Many people think those who hurt us need to earn our forgiveness. And others feel those who hurt us need to be willing to accept our forgiveness in order for us to forgive in the first place. Here is where I differ: I don't believe forgiveness is ever determined by the perpetrator, because when I forgive, it's for me. There is no attachment to toxic emotions or the harmful experience that took place. We deserve freedom and peace from those who hurt us, and from the experience they put us through.

Kate and I looked up the definition of *forgive* in *Webster's* dictionary and *bam!*—my TEDx Manhattan Beach Talk, "We Need a New Definition of Forgiveness," was born. Here's an excerpt:

I was standing on a rock high above the valley floor below, taking in the beauty, when unexpectedly, I felt a welcoming, deep sensation. For a second, I was conscious of how it would feel if I could let the anger, betrayal, and resentment release away—and it felt so *free*! I wanted this feeling to last forever. At that moment, I realized: I didn't want to hold on to this pain anymore. It was not serving me; it was harming me.[3]

Clarity comes in many forms. It may land in our hearts and souls by way of feelings, or in our minds by way of thoughts. We must listen to those "aha" moments! Standing on the rock, clarity began in my heart and soul when I felt a longing to be free of toxic emotions. I was no longer attached to my rage, sadness, and pain. Sinking into this possibility of forgiveness and self-love gave me freedom to distance myself from the toxic emotions my husband's betrayal caused. Being in this place of peace, I realized, "You have everything you need to survive—and thrive—leaving your marriage. You will be fine." That became the moment I decided to forgive *and* divorce my husband.

In step one, we discussed how parts of us from our past build upon one another to create the person we are today. In this chapter, we begin deep inner work and uncover *who that person is*. We will:

- Discover the values that make up who you are. Dive into this exercise with an open heart, mind, and soul. Finding your values leads to a daily practice of living life from your core—your truest self—without ever sacrificing your integrity or apologizing for who you are.

- Find the inner warrior that lives within each one of us, located in the solar plexus. When you attach to your confidence and personal power, while living in alignment with your values, your life becomes full of possibilities. As a reminder from step one, remember to let go of societal and self-inflicted pressures, to live your life in any way you choose.
- Honor your wounds. Everyone experiences hurt, pain, and loss. You must stop feeling shameful about your wounds. Honor your traumas and bring them into the light for healing.
- Celebrate you! Don't get caught up in what you'd like to or "should" change about yourself, forgetting to stop and acknowledge how great you already are. By consciously choosing joy and happiness, you elevate your energy.

Please take this chapter seriously and fully commit to doing the work. Transformation and healing can get messy and be difficult, exhausting, and frustrating. When it gets hard or you feel uncomfortable, use the five-part process I shared in step one to awaken your senses and have peace moments in nature.

Remember, you are worthy.

"Who are you?"

If I asked you this question, my guess is you would answer with something like, "I am a woman, father, yoga instructor, doctor, runner, survivor" . . . The list goes on and on. Yes, you are correct, those are parts of who you are. But those are labels.

Labels dictate what we do in this world—they do not define who we are.

For example, I can say I'm an author, speaker, coach, wilderness guide, mother, and many other labels. But when I show up to do this work day in and day out, what drives me to create successes and achievements? How can I be a friend or partner who steps into forgiveness? And what holds me accountable to be a good mom for my boys?

Our values are the core principles of who we are. When our values determine our decisions, life is created by our choosing. Imagine our values as inner compasses that we use to find our North Star. Some of my values are family, love, connection, joy, honesty, respect, nature, and many others. When my life feels out of alignment, I come back to my values and determine if I'm living from my heart, soul, and spirit.

Standing on the rock in Sequoia National Park, I realized life wasn't working with my husband because I wasn't living in my values. In the chaos of my husband's betrayal and addictions, I lost sight of my life and was living according to his. I had to forgive my husband for his betrayals, lies, and deceit, and I needed to forgive myself for allowing me to get to this place. Without forgiveness, we continue to live in judgment of ourselves and one another, creating turmoil in our lives. I also needed to let go of my label of wife and instead become a coparent, trusting that I could be alone and find *joy*, a value I hold deeply. Through this work, I will challenge you to let go of labels and instead live from your values. You will be shocked at how this simple practice can alter your life.

M

Let's start from the beginning. We are all pure human beings born into this world with a blank canvas—representing our life—to be painted however we choose. As infants, life is simple as we rely on others to take care of us. Experiences happen, and through trial and error we find out what we do and do not like. We learn and grow, painting our white canvas with successes, failures, and learning. Childhood, teen years, and young adult life come into play. Our decision making is influenced by teachers, friends, society, family, and perhaps our spiritual lives. Life can sometimes be confusing and hard as we struggle to find our way. Other times we may feel it's in the "flow," when we have an energized focus and things just happen. Without even realizing, we begin finding our values in our early years by determining what we feel is important.

For example, creativity became a core value in my life during senior year of high school. As a pregnant, misunderstood teenager, I longed to escape reality. Sick of judgment and feeling unheard, art became my sacred space for safety and freedom. My art teacher, Mr. Riepe, handed me a key to the studio and said, "Whenever you need to be here, it's yours." This became my safe haven, and paints, pencils, and mixed media became tools to create a life I could live in. Today, my writing, speaking, business, and personal life flows with creativity.

As we enter adulthood, our careers or roles in life may impact how we see or view the world and how it "works." Relationships deepen as we become more intimate with others. And friendships from our past may end as new connections begin. When and if we choose to find our life partner, we hope their values align with ours. When they do, we live in partnership according to our shared values, perhaps raising kids and building our lives in alignment.

When our shared values are no longer honored or understood, our marriages and relationships eventually collapse, causing breakups and divorce. Unless we know our values, how can we be sure our partners share ours? When we enter a relationship knowing our individual and shared values, we can work to deepen our understanding of each other and the relationship itself. I believe that had I known or understood my core values before getting married, I probably would have viewed my relationship differently, perhaps never getting married, thus avoiding the pain.

I encourage you to complete step two with those you care about: introduce it to your parents, friends, colleagues, and partners. I even share values work with my children. I encourage them to follow their dreams by aligning with their own values, not mine or society's. Getting back to the core of who we are will create a better world as a whole.

Discover Your Values and Who You Are

When I did values work at CTI (Coaches Training Institute), I found myself crying on the floor, feeling like I'd been punched in the stomach. I remember the conversation in my head and heart: *Oh my God. Going through what I have with David hurts so bad because when he lied, he stepped on my values of trust and honesty. I valued our family and marriage, and he didn't when he was with men. Where were our shared values of connection and communication when he was living a secret life?* My classmates were brilliant at "holding space," a concept that means being with someone without judgment while lending an ear, an open heart, and a shoulder to lean on.[4]

I needed support when I realized that not only had David stepped on my values during marriage but also I had pulled away from my own values. I had worked so hard at rebuilding trust with myself and others after my rape, and of course I believed I could trust my husband. Regardless, after having been violated in my past, why didn't I listen and trust myself when I felt something was "off" in our marriage?

The year prior to my husband's revelations, I was running on a hill while training. I fell to my knees in a sudden sobfest, crying for no apparent reason. A voice in my head said, *Sara, he is gay.* At the time I felt our marriage was in trouble and needed work, but I'd never have expected he had been living a lie. The voice was so clear it was as if God were speaking into my head and heart. I picked myself up after a few minutes of crying and didn't speak about what happened until months later. When I finally found the courage to share with David, he said, "I love you and would never cheat on you," and I believed him.

Why didn't I listen to myself, to that inner voice, and push harder to find the truth? Why didn't I trust my intuition? I now know why: I didn't want my intuition to be right. Ultimately, this is an area where I have learned to forgive myself.

There are two important reasons people live inauthentic lives or lives that are not of their choosing:

1. *Unidentified values.* As mentioned earlier, understanding your values is like having your heart and soul be a compass that points to the North Star, your life. When leading with your values, you will stay on the trail. But you must be clear about what's important to you to live a life of your choosing. And to have it be a life you love.

2. *Unaware or unwilling to listen.* This was me. Many times I noticed red flags or had a feeling in the pit of my stomach that something was off. This was my intuition speaking to me, but I didn't listen. Perhaps it was due to fear of having to face what scared me most. Or because I chose to honor what I thought was our shared value of marriage over my own value of trust. Whatever the case, unless you begin to listen to your heart, soul, mind, and spirit instead of outward voices, you will never be completely aligned, aware, and ready to live your best life. A great way to begin listening is by meditating in nature. Just sit, be still, with your hands over your heart chakra, close your eyes, and listen. Be mindful of what appears in your thoughts and feelings. You can even go back to the five-part process for peace moments introduced at the end of the previous chapter.

During your time working on step two, please know that I am committed to holding space for you as your own clarity manifests and "aha" moments enlighten you. Have your journal and pen ready as I lead you through a short, guided visualization. Then we'll talk through the process of discovering your values.

Guided Visualization for Finding Your Values

Let's begin once again by grounding ourselves in nature. Imagine yourself sinking into the earth. Place your hands over your heart.
Close your eyes.
Take a deep breath in, hold, and release.

Smell the air.

Feel the ground beneath you. And thank Mother Earth for holding space for you.

Now, take notice of your body.

Where are you holding tension? Your shoulders? Legs? Maybe even in your toes. Begin to allow those parts of your body to release any anxiety, settling into the earth below you.

Continue to breathe with your hands over your heart.

One by one, take notice of the thoughts that appear in your mind.

Begin to imagine a swarm of butterflies coming in. Place a thought on each butterfly and allow them to be carried away.

Take a deep breath in. And release your breath.

You are in this moment—without judgment.

Take another deep breath in. Be here. In peace.

Release your breath.

Go to a time and place in life when you have felt completely happy and aligned. This could be your first memory in life, or perhaps it was an experience from today.

A peak moment when everything felt as though it was as it should be.

What was happening around you?

Continue to breathe with your eyes closed and allow yourself to go back to that moment.

What made this moment so great?

What was the weather like? Were there any smells you noticed?

Pay attention to the details around you.

Who was with you?

What emotions are happening with those around you? And within you?

Take another breath in and release.

Allow this moment to come to life, as if it's happening right now.

Take in a breath from the deepest place within you.

And release.

Feel into this moment you chose as the time and place when life felt really good. When you felt in alignment with who you truly are.

Stay here for as long as you like.

Just breathe.

When you are ready, begin coming back to the present time and place.

Wiggle your fingers and toes.

Open your eyes and remain in this peaceful moment.

Allow Mother Earth and nature to continue holding space for you. Hold this good place within you as you work on finding your core values from this experience.

After the meditation and when you're ready, pick up your journal and free write about your peak moment. Set a timer for five minutes and, without stopping, journal everything that comes to you. Detail what was happening during the moment. Write about the people who were there, how you were feeling, and why it was an aligned moment in your life.

Let me share a peak moment I had with clients in the Grand Canyon in July 2019. We were on a five-day, coed retreat. Before every retreat, I ask what gifts each client brings to the group, which I talk about in step three. Lucky for us, in this group Nick shared he was a drummer.

On day two, we decided to hike up a creek bed to a small waterfall in a side canyon. Wading through the water, I encouraged everyone to pay attention to the tadpoles, frogs, and beautiful slabs of rock embracing us on either side. Playing and exploring are things I want my clients to do.

We reached the falls and sat under the flowing water, allowing it to wash over us. Eventually, I called the group together into a circle. Sitting on rocks in the shallow end of the creek with the falls behind us, I asked Nick to lead us in a drum circle, using rocks as our instruments. It was a beautiful, intimate, and authentic moment. Together in rhythm with our hearts, we created music that echoed in the slot canyon and through Phantom Creek. Looking up, I saw smiles and peace moments float through everyone as they were brought back to their child-like state. One client even experienced his first peace moment, which delighted me. Nothing else mattered in the world but the ten of us, creating melody.

<hr/>

We remember people or experiences by how they make us feel. If the peak experience you wrote about didn't intimately and emotionally touch your heart and soul, please read or listen to the guided meditation again.

A popular saying goes, "Your beliefs become your thoughts.

Your thoughts become your words. Your words become your actions. Your actions become your habits. Your habits become your values. Your values become your destiny."[5] You want to get to the heartbeat of what moves you: ultimately, this becomes your destiny.

Now let's dig into finding your core values through a five-part process.

1. **EXTRACT YOUR VALUES.** Now that you've written about a peak experience, pull out the values that made it so important. What values were being honored? Looking back at my peak experience in the canyon, it's fair to say that connection, nature, intimacy, love, creativity, inspiration, and adventure are a few of my values. List as many values as you can. You may have to come back to this part after further exploration of your peak moment.

2. **GROUP YOUR VALUES AND FIND THEIR THEMES.** You are looking for your core values, those you will use to live and make decisions on a daily basis. Keep your number of core values between five and ten. If you have too few values, you're not honoring every part of you. Too many values, and you're watering down the many parts of you.

   Find common themes and group your values. For example, if I had truth, honesty, responsibility, and fairness on my list, I would group those together under the heading "honesty." My belief is that honesty must run through the heartbeat of everything in order for anything to be true

3. **CREATE VALUE STATEMENTS.** Using words from each group, create a statement that supports and provides

context for the value. For example: *Honesty* holds people responsible for their actions, thus creating fairness in relationships.

4. **RANK YOUR VALUES.** This step may require you to revisit your list daily until you feel comfortable with where your values are ranked.

5. **TEST YOUR VALUES ON A DAILY BASIS.** Ask yourself these questions:

    —How do they make you feel?

    —What is your life like, or will it be like, when living according to your values?

    —Are they personal to you?

    —Do you see any values that are inconsistent with who you are?

Your core values guide you to live daily with intention, awareness, and alignment in who you are. Choices and decision making will become easier, and life will feel in the flow. As you continue to test your values, deepen and grow them by returning to the guided visualization. Remember that as you learn, heal, and transform in life, your values may shift.

Embrace the Greatest Love in Your Life: Your Inner Warrior

We all have an internal power and wisdom within us, emanating from our solar plexus. I like to call this our "inner warrior." We can access him or her at any time. Learning how to tap into this strength and energy gives us the confidence and courage to do what we never thought possible. It also allows us to become someone we never envisioned or imagined.

I often call on my inner warrior and have drawn on her strength to make big decisions, such as when I chose to keep my son, decided against all odds to attend college, and made the decision to write this book. And when I've been questioned in life, my inner warrior, her voice and wisdom, has reminded me of my purpose.

My inner warrior was put to the test on New Year's Eve 2017. Entering a house party full of married couples, sans partner, was something I was still getting used to. Having been in a marriage where my husband was the spotlight of our relationship, it took a while for me to learn how to step into a social life—alone. My coping mechanism was to attend late and slip in after everyone arrived. Climbing the stairs and walking into the crowd, I thought to myself, *Okay, here we go! You can do this.*

I was sharing details of my life with three other women, one of whom had been drinking quite a bit. Her judgmental gaze eyed me up and down. Suddenly she asked, "So, I have to ask. Do you have qualifications to write a book or do this work? Are you a therapist? What background do you have? Who are you that you think you can do this?" I stood dumbfounded, shocked, and silent. Her words stung and hurt. The other women began nervously defending me. I wanted to flee and leave, but instead I chose to take a breath and connect with the wisdom, strength, and calm of my inner warrior. After explaining my certifications and education, I excused myself and went to the bathroom. Looking in the mirror, I saw a woman who was still reeling from the pain in her past. I said, "Thank you for doing the work, Sara. You are deepening your self-love and self-worth."

I carried that conversation home with me and woke up the

next morning feeling uneasy. Part of me wished I'd have gotten angry and defended myself more than I had. This bothered me even more than the conversation itself. I'm not an angry woman, and toxic emotions aren't something I like to hold.

Grabbing my stand-up paddleboard, I went in the Pacific Ocean and thought about what happened the night prior. I realized that the universe, God, and spirit provide us with the lessons and learnings we need. In my moment of clarity on the water, I understood the conversation had handed me a powerful reminder. Like many others have in the past, the woman judged and questioned my worth, identity, and knowledge, projecting her own insecurities in the process. This was her work that needed to be done. I chose not to judge this woman for the conversation, or me for my lessons. Was I worthy of writing a book? A better question: Is the world worthy of hearing others' stories in order to heal, grow, learn, and be inspired to create a better life? I think so.

For many of us, especially those who have lived through relational and betrayal trauma, our self-worth and self-love are values we need to rebuild and work on daily. My self-worth was at an all-time low after my husband's betrayal, and to be honest, I didn't even realize how little I had. Because of my husband's narcissism, he at times manipulated situations within our marriage, in a way that made me feel wrong. This happened more often during the final few years, when he was deep in his addictions. And because I am an empath who valued marriage, I took on responsibility for things that weren't even mine. Many nights I'd lie in bed wondering why I felt distant from the man lying next to me. When I questioned my husband, his general answer was, "I'm busy with work. I have a lot of stress to provide for the family." Naturally, I did what I could to ease his life by keeping the house clean, making dinners, and managing the kids, their schedules, and our home. My hope was that by relieving him of stress, he'd find energy to focus on our relationship.

When that didn't happen, I would only try harder. A popular definition of insanity is "doing the same thing over and over again but expecting different results."[6] This toxic cycle and dysfunctional way of living caused me to ask, "What's wrong with me?" Hence, my self-worth suffered.

It would take two years of intense emotional and psychological work to make sense of our seventeen-year marriage. I had to learn to forgive myself for only seeing my husband's beautiful, brilliant light, not his shadow part. Many people in these kinds of relationships are blinded by their partner's light—and what partner wants to see their significant other's shadow part?

This is a responsibility I hold, and I have learned to forgive myself. Calling on my inner warrior, I work on self-worth and self-love every single day. The hard-core truth about relationship and betrayal trauma is this: after years of lies, deception, manipulation, and confusion, it's far easier to believe in others than in yourself. Self-worth and self-love are so important, I made them step three in this book.

Let me share a story from the trail about a client who also lived through relational and betrayal trauma. As you read, use her experience as a metaphor and think about how you relate within your own life. When have you felt like you couldn't take one more step, yet needed to—perhaps to survive?

Hiking out of the canyon on a hot day in July, Eva called

on her inner warrior for strength. Tired and emotional, she desperately wanted to finish the day strong. But mind-numbing voices questioned her abilities, causing an internal struggle that fed negative self-worth. Eva's inner critic was beating her down. The more attention she gave her exhaustion and doubt, the more difficult the journey became.

As her guide, I never questioned Eva's physical capability to hike out of the canyon. Her breakdown on the trail was about more than being hot and spent. She was healing from past relationships, facing self-criticism, and answering her own question: "Who am I?"

An empathetic woman of service, Eva launched Project Kindle in 1998, a nonprofit summer camp for children impacted by HIV/AIDS. And twenty years later, in this vast canyon, she was focused on her own healing. I'll share Eva's experience in her own words.

We were an hour back on the trail after taking a rest, and I was hot! I started to cry. I was so out of breath! Each step was taking more of my replenished energy. It was as if we had never stopped at all. I took one step at a time and just cried and cried and cried.

Sara calmly and supportively pointed out that I wasn't just crying because this sucked . . . though it did. I was releasing the pain, self-doubt, and uncertainty I had stored up over my life. Step after step, I was crying out all of the trauma from my past. My body had no more will to hold on to anything but my actual life. It had to use my trauma energy to keep me physically moving—I could no longer hold on to it.

Sara saw my pattern of fear and self-doubt—and she

helped me to see it too. This was a deep-rooted fear that I wasn't good enough. It was the voice in my head that was telling me, *Eva, you suck—you can't do this. What are you thinking? You suck, you suck, you suck.* That is what I was hearing over and over and over again.

Sara asked me to find an affirmation. I came up with something I knew I needed, but didn't believe at the moment. I replied, "I am strong." Sara had me say it with each step. I. Am. Strong. I said those words out loud again, and again, and again until I had no more tears to cry and the emotional component of the hike was shed. Now I could be strong and do whatever possible to get myself out of this canyon.

I did the only thing I knew how to do in that moment of utter relinquishment. I prayed. I thanked God, spirit, and the universe for this entire experience. I was truly grateful I said yes to this adventure, which so synchronistically came to pass.[7]

Connecting with your inner warrior gives you strength to live life according to your values. Eva struggled with fear, self-doubt, criticism, uncertainty, and a lack of voice. She was also a single mom to six kids and the founder of an important non-profit. She was really good at taking care of everyone but needed to do the same for herself. Though an outwardly happy person, she longed to find freedom and peace from her past. And to once again find courage and confidence to do big things in this world.

As Eva climbed up the trail, she had no choice but to face her barriers and struggles. The pain and struggles she carried were finally ready to be released. But to overcome these barriers and climb the trail, she needed to access her strength and inner wisdom. By using the affirmation "I am strong" during her hike, she became more resilient with every step, while also connecting with her inner warrior. In turn, her self-worth and self-love deepened as a woman, as a survivor of relationship trauma, and as a single mom of six children. I'll share more about Eva's experience later in this book. To witness her transformation was a gift, one of the most beautiful testaments of surrendering and faith I have ever witnessed.

Many of you are held back from achieving your goals and dreams because of fear. Perhaps you're afraid of failure, making mistakes, or being seen. Add that nasty inner critic, who tells you you're unworthy of those goals and dreams, and success becomes more unlikely. This is why your inner warrior is so important. He or she gives you permission to smash barriers, step out of your comfort zone, and create a life you love. But you can also learn from failure. So the only question to ask is, "What is possible?" Please have your journal ready as you dive into a seven-part process to connect with your inner warrior.

Connect with Nature and Your Root Chakra

You've been reading about your seven chakras, nature, and spiritual energy throughout this book. Your inner warrior resides in your solar plexus. That said, as a trauma survivor, I've found that to access my strength and personal power, it was first necessary to connect with my root chakra, which, not surprisingly, has energy originating from the earth element. From your root chakra we imagine our lives as tree roots growing into the earth while grounding, creating safety, and fostering expansion in our lives. Connecting with your inner warrior means setting aside distractions and once again going into nature. I'd like to guide you through a meditation to find and connect with your inner warrior—the heartbeat of who you are.

Guided Meditation to Find Your Inner Warrior

Take a moment to sit in a space in nature, or imagine
yourself in nature, and close your eyes.

Feel the earth below you, holding you.

Take a deep breath in. And exhale.

Begin to notice your breath and start to slow every inhale
and exhale.

What does it feel like to relax your body as you breathe out?
Where can you release further?

Allow your breath to soften your physical body and mind
into a space of calm. A space of peace. A space where
you are held.

Imagine yourself sitting at the bottom of a canyon, a deep,
narrow valley created by forces of nature over time. Feel
your body held by the ancient ground below you. And
witness the majesty of the towering canyon walls around
you, holding you in this safe and wondrous place.

What else do you see? What can you observe here in
this space in nature? Even with the massive rocks
surrounding you, what little details can you take in?
A grain of sand? A slowly drifting cloud? A heart-
shaped rock?

What can you hear? Is there wind or is it silent? Can you
hear your own breath? Can you hear your own heartbeat?

As you take in the magnificence of this space, you sense an energy approaching you. Although it's walking toward you from the greatness of the canyon, it's also not outside yourself. You sense that it's a part of you that has decided to return home to you. This presence is your inner warrior.

As your inner warrior comes closer, you begin to notice what it looks like. What it feels like. Where in your body do you feel the energy, strength, and power of your inner warrior? What are the sensations? Notice where your power lives in you as you share space with this elevated presence.

Your inner warrior sits next to you and asks if you have any questions. What do you want to know?

You ask your inner warrior, "What do I need to learn?" "What is my purpose?" "What am I here to do?" "How can I use my values to move forward with my dreams?"

Your inner warrior nods its head. It looks at you and says, "The answers to these questions live within you. Listen to your first instinct. That instinct is my answer. Your instinct is me. I've always been here. I've never left you. I will always be here to guide you. You have to trust your gut."

This inner warrior is everything you look up to. It's everything you desire to be and feel. It's everything you dream of becoming.

Yet you have a knowing, a true belief, that the answers to your deepest questions are already within. Even when you have doubts, trust that your instincts and your heart will guide you in the right direction.

As your inner warrior begins to fade, the energy of this
wisdom begins to swirl and rests in the palms of your
hands. You place your hands on your heart and feel the
answers resting inside yourself.

Trust that you can return to this inner warrior at any time.
This inner warrior is a part of you. This inner warrior
is you.

Take a deep breath into your heart. And release the breath,
removing doubt and obstacles to the answers you seek,
as you exhale.

As you sit in the stillness of the present moment, begin to
feel yourself resting on the earth. And when you feel
ready, bring movement back to your hands and feet and
slowly open your eyes.

Journal about this experience. What was it like to be with
your inner warrior? What were the answers to the questions you asked:

- What do I need to learn?
- What is my purpose?
- What am I here to do?
- How can I use my values to move forward with
  my dreams?

Notice where your powerful inner warrior lives within
your body. How will you call on your inner warrior, voice,
and strength on your road to healing and forgiveness?

Who and What Are You Willing to Fight for and Defend?

You have a warrior heart. What or who do you believe in so deeply that you will fight to the ends of the earth? For example, I will always be there for my children and family. I believe in guiding my boys to create dreams and a destiny aligned with their values, gifts, and purpose in this world.

> Take a few moments in your journal and finish this sentence:
> I believe deeply in _____.

Call on and Surround Yourself with Other Warriors

This can be difficult. Your friends, family, and inner circle may shift as you grow stronger. Look for people who will defend and fight for what you believe in. Stay open to those who see you and your purpose and want to stand beside you.

Conquer Your Fears

Living happens when you face what scares you most. Confront and conquer the barriers holding you back. Overcoming one barrier builds your ability to do it again . . . and again . . . and again. Soon you won't think twice about living boldly as a warrior, aligned with your values and your unpressured choices.

Let's use Eva's story as an example. As she hiked up the trail, her inner critic fed her negative self-worth: *Eva, you suck, you can't do this. What are you thinking? You suck, you suck, you suck.* Transformation began the second she connected with her inner warrior and the words *I am strong*. The more she recited her mantra, the more her belief in self-worth deepened.

Also, it's important to recognize that many times people mistake excitement for fear because these emotions manifest in the body much the same way. Your heart and pulse race, you may feel sweaty, and for me, it's hard to sit still. By differentiating how your body responds to each emotion, you can determine whether you're facing fear or excitement. Remember that when you avoid the necessary, you're running from what is possible. Many things in life can get hard. But in the "hard" is where your relationship to yourself strengthens, and you find your greatest "aha," magical moments. We'll dive more into this in step five: when the work gets hard, stay present.

Embrace the Callings of Your Heart and Work on You

Plain and simple: pursue the desires of your heart and soul. Every day do more of what makes you happy. Take a walk. Sit in nature. Write. Read a poem. Go to yoga, swim, walk the beach. I encourage my clients to create a vision board every six months. A vision board is a collage of images, words, pictures, and affirmations used to clarify and focus on one's dreams, goals, and desires. You are the artist of your life—your board is a source of inspiration and motivation.

Love Deeply and Openly

Without love, darkness prevails. You will hear me say this again and again: *the most important relationship you can have in life is with yourself.* Love yourself so deeply that you will never forsake your truth, integrity, and commitment to who you are. Nor will you follow a path to someone else's dreams in place of your own.

Be authentic and vulnerable with your heart. In place of judgment, when noticing your flaws or wrongdoings, shower yourself with love and fierce self-compassion, and remind yourself, "I am doing the best that I can in every given moment."

Be Adventurous

You're called to live deeply and openly, and to take healthy risks. Being brave and living an adventurous life doesn't mean we're all called to climb mountains. Perhaps you're led to pursue a new career, move across the country, or build a new relationship. Whatever the adventure, embrace it.

My hope is that you continue working and playing with your inner warrior, inviting her/him into your everyday practice of living by choice. The more you do this, the less your inner critic will get in the way of your dreams, goals, and aspirations. When I feel myself sitting in doubt or despair, I call on my inner warrior, knowing she is available to me at any time. You can do the same with your inner warrior.

Honor Your Wounds

For years, I only spoke about my rape with those closest to me. Though I had stepped into forgiveness for me and my perpetrator, I assumed that sharing my experience would make others uncomfortable. I wasn't interested in creating turmoil where none existed. What I failed to realize is how many people it would have helped, had I faced my assumptions and shared my story. Since speaking out, more and more women and men have come forward with their own experiences of sexual assault. I've met women who became pregnant as a result, and men who had never spoken of what happened to them.

While we don't need to share every detail of our lives, giving ourselves permission to speak our truth gives others the opportunity to listen. By honoring our wounds and bringing them into the light, we give others permission to do the same. In doing so, we are healing communities filled with trauma and pain, and breaking patterns that have caused toxic behaviors in society for way too long.

Celebrate You

We are all perfectly imperfect. And with that imperfection we're given permission to celebrate who we are at this moment. When you feel hesitant to focus on your own joy and happiness, reaffirm your values and call on your inner warrior. We all deserve to laugh, dance, sing, and be who we choose to be in this lifetime. Enjoy the moments while walking to your destination. I promise you, by celebrating along the way, your heart will open to greater manifestations than you ever imagined. And your desire to forgive will awaken.

Turn the page and continue the work in step three, where you'll learn about self-worth and self-love. In the process, get ready to love yourself like never before.

Embrace Self-Worth + Self-Love

E ven though I love exploring self-worth and self-love with clients, starting this chapter was difficult. I found myself typing paragraphs and deleting them several times. I wanted to share so many things, yet barriers—and my inner critic—weren't allowing me to express my thoughts and feelings. Frustration took over as I spiraled down a rabbit hole, questioning my worthiness when I didn't complete my writing deadline before leaving on a Grand Canyon retreat. My ego wanted to pass judgment on my mind. But my heart chose to release expectations and trust the words would flow when the time was right.

Standing on the rim of the canyon the night before guiding my group of men and women in, I looked into the vastness below and asked for guidance: *Mother Nature and canyon spirits, please provide signs for self-worth and self-love during this retreat that I can share with my readers.* The canyon experience delivered. Now, two days home after guiding one of the most powerful groups through forty-seven miles of trails, storytelling from this retreat will guide you through step three: embracing self-worth and self-love. When we trust the universe and creative process, endless possibilities reveal themselves.

In step two, we explored *who you are* by uncovering your values and inner warrior. This step will provide you with spiritual and personal development insight to connect with your self-worth and self-love. You will:

- Find and connect with your heart. Your heart beats about 100,000 times in one day and about 35 million times in a year. During an average lifetime, the human heart beats more than 2.5 billion times.[1] To love and value yourself, you must connect with the heartbeat of who you are.
- View what does not (and does) determine your self-worth. Too many times we attach our worthiness to others or to material items. Let's go back to what matters most: you.
- Have a conversation with your inner critic. Your critical voice sabotages your relationships and possibilities, ultimately preventing you from living your best life. By fostering self-worth and self-love, you live life on your terms—with freedom, peace, love, and forgiveness—while silencing your inner critic.

We returned late in the evening from an inspiring, emotional, and physically demanding retreat. Eleven humans adventured trails, walked through creeks, went deep into their personal relationships, shared stories, and gained moments of clarity. I believe in authentic leadership, which requires my vulnerability. Holding space for five nights and six days while exposing a bit of myself can be exhausting, even as much as I love my work.

Turning off the car engine, I took a deep breath before unloading my hiking packs and walking into the house. I used to hate this part of the trip. Not because I was coming home to my boys, but because I wasn't coming home to a partner. Sometimes after retreats I would sit in my room and cry gut-wrenching tears because of an overwhelming loneliness. I wanted someone to welcome and embrace me when I entered the door, saying, "Tell me everything, down to the smallest detail." I didn't need this, but I longed for it.

My worthiness and love aren't tied to another human being, nor should they be. However, I value the power of intimacy and conversations within a partner relationship, something my personal life has been void of for far too long. Many times people turn to their daughters, sons, friends, parents, or family members to fill missing parts of their lives. But in a relationship, no one should be responsible for playing a role that isn't theirs. Your child should never replace your spouse, just as a parent should never replace your partner. If you highlight anything in this chapter, let it be this: *by developing your self-worth and self-love, you deepen and welcome healthy relationships in your life.*

I've noticed more people pushing aside and excusing their inevitable longing for partnerships while filling their void for intimacy with alcohol, drugs, or other unhealthy sources. This self-destructive behavior can complicate one's development of self-worth and self-love.

Recently, I spoke with my father about this, and it struck a chord. It's a sad story, but worth sharing.

One Christmas morning my boys and I were at church. For some reason unbeknownst to me, I couldn't stop crying as our cantor sang "Ave Maria," his voice filling the space. I felt something was wrong, yet I was oddly at peace. After mass, I inexplicably knelt in prayer and lit a candle while my boys walked out to the car. I prayed for God to be with anyone going through a difficult time over the holidays. Not fifteen minutes later, my boys and I returned home to find that our sweet dog, Barkley, had passed away while we were at church.

Looking back, I have no doubt that while I was crying and feeling at peace, Barkley was leaving this earth. It was devastating to lose him. Sadness, rage, loss, and anger swept over me as I, once again, had to deal with a traumatic situation without a partner. I didn't handle it well. My brain flooded with all of the times I've had to be the strong one in my family, making quick decisions in the face of tragedy. As I cradled Barkley in my arms, I wept for all of the times I'd been there before, holding on to what I had no control over and couldn't protect. And then having to let go.

My boys stood there, shocked, asking me to pull myself together. I couldn't do it. What started out as an okay Christmas ended in a flood of realizations and loss. I'd been working on my personal development and healing for so long, and I was tired of being in this life alone.

That afternoon, my dad called me to check in. I broke down crying and professed how it sucked not to have anyone there with me during trying times. He said, "You are never alone. Look at all of the people who love you. You've got us." I felt angry. This ingrained cycle of leaning on others to fill an empty space in my heart needed to be addressed. Taking a pause with my dad, I explained how neither he, Mom, me, nor anyone else would ever fulfill the role a partner is meant to fulfill. No amount of love from others or numbing out could fix my longing at that moment. I assured him that, yes, I'm happy and have never loved myself more deeply. Yet, while loving and honoring ourselves and our relationships, it's also all right to say, "I want and am ready for more." My dad, the first man I loved, responded, "I get it. I hear you. And I'm sorry. I wish I could do more."

This conversation was a necessary step in breaking past patterns within my tight-knit family, who likes to try to make everything okay. Sometimes your only job is to hold space and say, "I see you."

Before we proceed, I'd like to guide you through a simple practice of connecting with your heart chakra and accepting the self-love that flows through each of us. I use this short prayer with clients, and I encourage you to wake every morning reciting these words. If you can, please sit or lie on the ground. If not, sit in a comfortable space indoors, with your feet on the floor.

Place your hands over your heart and close your eyes. Take a deep breath in, filling your lungs with air. Release your breath.

Feel your heartbeat. Listen to the natural rhythm that is created. Your heart picked you before any other internal organ. Acknowledge your heart and say these words aloud. After each verse, pause and listen to what your heart speaks in return.

> *My dearest heart,*
> *I see you.*
> *I hear you.*
> *I feel you.*
> *I love you.*
> *My dearest heart, please continue flowing your love through me.*

Love is the energy of connecting people, animals, beings, and nature. Love and worthiness flow from your heart and soul when you live daily in alignment with your values. Without understanding self-love and self-worth from your heart, authentic relationships cannot be created and deep connections cannot be forged. When this happens, you may resort to attaching worthiness and love to material items—cars, houses, degrees—in place of what truly matters: intimacy with family, friends, and a partnership. Most important, without love, you will never find forgiveness.

hr

After a long day of hiking in the Grand Canyon, my colead breathwork meditation coach, Jenna Reiss, and I decided to have our group's evening breathwork and coaching session inside the cabin. The group was sharing their experiences and having an open dialogue afterward. One of our clients moved me when she said, "For the first time in my life, I felt my heart beat during breathwork. I didn't even know I had a heart." Putting her hands over her chest, she grasped for words as she expressed what it was like to actually feel! Looking around the room, the empathy and love from others was open and inviting. Scars and tears on our client's heart from years of abuse were slowly mending and healing because of the collective love of these people who were once strangers and because of this experience she was having.

Our hearts are our most precious gift. It bewilders me how our hearts can endure hardships, recover from pain, feel raw emotions, and love so deeply. In fact, when faced with severe stress, whether physical or emotional, our hearts can relay symptoms similar to those of a heart attack. This is called takotsubo cardiomyopathy, otherwise known as broken-heart syndrome, and was first described in 1990 in Japan.[2] Though you can recover from a broken heart with no long-term heart damage, many of us have heard of partners choosing to die naturally because of overwhelming emotional pain and sadness from the loss of a loved one. Love—and our hearts—is full of wonder and awe.

As an embryo in your mother's womb, your heart was the first internal organ formed. It beat within you as your mother's continued beating within her. Experiences, emotions, and thoughts flowed through her mind, body, heart, and soul—and many of those messages were delivered to you. This dynamic was about more than hearing her heartbeat and whatever music she might play to her belly; you also received chemical signals through the placenta.[3] It's wild to think that your mother's experiences in the outside world essentially became yours in the inside world of her body.

Professor Catherine Monk and her colleagues "study the long reach of prenatal influences, especially among women who suffer from depression, stress, and anxiety. They found that some fetuses register mothers' stress, and that fetal reactivity correlates with infant temperament at four months old."[4] Monk stated, "The pregnant female communicates to her offspring cues about what the postnatal world is like, and the adaptation starts in utero."[5]

I think of my firstborn son and the stresses he must have endured as I recovered from my trauma of sexual assault. The sadness, rage, loss, fear, and anxiety that flowed through me also flowed through my son. Have I thought about how this affected him? Yes, for sure. I've had to forgive myself for things I couldn't control, such as bringing him into the world under those circumstances, and not being able to stop my rapist from attempting this on another woman. I've also forgiven myself for mistakes I made as a mom. Because safety became my first priority during my pregnancy and after his birth, I was far more of a "helicopter mom" with him than I was with my second or third son. Our relationship had years of struggle because of my anxiety and control issues. Thankfully, I've learned better and now do better.

As women and mothers, we must give ourselves compassion and grace, and remember that we're human beings doing our best in the moment. Self-worth and self-love begin with our own heartbeats—and in the end, love wins.

In this step, I encourage you to regain the self-worth and self-love you strive for. Hold yourself tenderly throughout this section and know that you are loved without judgment.

What Does *Not* Determine Your Self-Worth

Please grab your journal and complete this statement:
My worthiness is not determined by _____.

Did you have trouble answering that question? In our society, many people determine self-worth with outward measures—your social circle, number of social media followers, physical appearance, and so forth—comparing themselves to others. I'd like to flip the script and help you view self-worth differently.

First, I'd like to focus on what *does not* determine your self-worth, so you can have a clearer understanding of what *does*.

- YOUR NUMBER OF FRIENDS. It's not about the number of friends you have in life—it's about the depth and intimacy of your relationships. As I have aged, my number of friends has decreased. That said, the connections I have with friends in my inner circle are deeper than ever. If I sense something isn't working, I open a dialogue, communicate thoughts, gather understanding, realign our love for each other, and lean in to the worthiness of our friendship.
- YOUR HOME. Whether in a tent on a summit or living in a multimillion-dollar home, I am the same person. Worthiness shouldn't be attached to the walls, or lack of walls, you live in.
- YOUR NET WORTH. The dollar does not keep you alive—your heart does. You cannot put a price tag on your heart and soul, or their worthiness.

- YOUR EDUCATION. Life is a textbook. Though formal education is important, I don't view those without diplomas or degrees as less worthy. My fortunate journey to live in a country where free education is available to all doesn't make me more worthy than those who lack such opportunity.

- YOUR APPEARANCE. I've been judged for my appearance and it sucks. I've heard, "I just thought you were one of those moms who had it all together. You are beautiful and work out. You have great kids and live in a big home. Little did I know!" Am I more worthy because of my appearance? Heck no. My worthiness stems from how I treat myself, and how I allow others to treat me.

- YOUR OCCUPATION. Do what you do with passion and purpose. And if you don't like what you're doing, you have the power to change course. Our world needs everything from CEOs to janitors. One is not more worthy than the other. People who value themselves and their role will spread love and value throughout their workplace.

I'm reminded of Dr. Martin Luther King Jr.'s speech "What Is Your Life's Blueprint?," in which he said, "If it falls your lot to be a street sweeper, sweep streets like Michelangelo painted pictures, sweep streets like Beethoven composed music, sweep streets like Leontyne Price sings before the Metropolitan Opera. Sweep streets like Shakespeare wrote poetry. Sweep streets so well that all the hosts of heaven and earth will have to pause and say: Here lived a great street sweeper who swept his job well. If you can't be a pine at the top of the hill, be a shrub in the valley. Be the best little shrub on the side of the hill."[6]

- OTHER PEOPLE. Other people don't determine your worthiness. Their opinions, judgments, and thoughts shouldn't impact how you view yourself. If your relationships are healthy, your self-worth will deepen. Keep that in mind when choosing whom you let into your life.

Self-worth flows from our solar plexus and is manifested and created by one person in this world: you. The more you focus on your internal core values from step two, and what you do have—by living in gratitude—the more your worthiness deepens and grows. Of course, surrounding yourself with people who appreciate who you are and what you have to offer helps. There's something about being with those you align with that gives you permission to expose your vulnerabilities and authentic self.

Prior to meeting at a retreat, I gather the group on a series of video conference calls, where we introduce ourselves and start our deep work. One of the first questions I ask is, "What personal gifts do you bring to this group?" Usually silence and quizzical looks follow this question. After a bit of thought, we dive into what we see as gifts: humor, kindness, joy, support, love, empathy, music, dance, and so forth. Someone inevitably says, "I never thought of myself as having gifts."

I have realized that we all view our internal gifts differently. Some of us are conditioned to believe our gifts are unworthy of being shared. Others feel as though they're burdening people with what they have to give. My hope is for us to set aside personal judgments on how our deepest gifts "should" be used, and instead allow others to receive what we have to offer. When seeing our internal gifts and sharing with others, we cultivate self-worth and self-love.

I'd like to share an example from when a mother and daughter joined us on a retreat. Throughout our time together, I encouraged each of them to dig deep individually while also nurturing their relationship. Going around the room during a group coaching session inside the cabin, we shared our stories and how we view ourselves. What struck me was how critical the mom was of herself. And what gave me hope was her daughter's reaction to this self-perception. I asked the two of them to sit knee to knee, holding hands while making eye contact, and share what they saw in each other. Their imaginary curtain raised as honest and truthful thoughts were delivered.

The daughter said to her mom, "Thank you for being you. Thank you for being my role model and best friend. I am who I am today because of you and the amazing person you are. You are kind, thoughtful, and a light to everyone you encounter. I love you more than you could ever imagine." What a gift for a mom to hear those words.

"I had no idea you felt this way," the mom said.

"Mom, you are a f***ing badass. I want you to see what we see."

We all learned the power of support, communication, love, intimacy, and understanding by being a part of this moment. In the process, both mother and daughter, individually and together, deepened their self-worth and self-love. So now I ask you, in relating to this experience: What gifts do you bring into this world?

No two humans are alike, so why compare yourself to others? What sets you apart is also what makes you unique, amazing, and worthy. While guiding on any given trail, I only see me for being me. I am not Alex Honnold, Cheryl Strayed, or Emma Rowena Gatewood (look them up if you haven't heard of them). Frankly, I wouldn't want to be them any more than they would want to be me. Your worthiness isn't based on free soloing El Capitan, hiking the Pacific Crest Trail, or solo hiking the Appalachian Trail at age sixty-seven. You are worthy through seeing your faults, learning from mistakes, feeding your gifts, and living life to the fullest in the process. At times on the trail, I have pushed limits or thought about different choices I could have made. In those moments, my self-worth has been fed by what life had to teach me. If you focus on what you didn't do right or if you consistently compare yourself to others with a "they could've done it better" attitude, you'll never step into the best version of yourself. And ultimately, the world needs the best version of you. Give yourself grace and compassion to love you for being you. The good. The difficult to swallow. And the indifferent.

> Let's revisit the journal prompt and see if you need to modify this important statement:
>
> My worthiness is not determined by _____.

Place your hands over your heart, take in a deep breath, and feel your heartbeat. Connect with your energy and love. Read your answers aloud, beginning with the statement, "My worthiness is not determined by . . ."

Now writing from your heart and not your mind, please complete this statement:

> My self-worth is honored when _____.

65

Placing your hands over your heart again, take in a deep breath, and feel your heartbeat against your body. Connect with your energy and love. Read your answers aloud, beginning with the statement, "My self-worth is honored when . . ."

We all need to understand what *does not* determine our self-worth as much as we need to notice what *does*. Please come back to this part of step three whenever you need reminders.

Pay Attention to the Narrative in Your Head

Going through my Wilderness First Responder training at the age of forty-one was brutal. But it was necessary in order to obtain my Commercial Use Authorization in the Grand Canyon and launch my business. I was scared for many reasons. What if I looked like an idiot in front of all those younger people? What if I failed?

I'll never forget my instructor standing behind me, screaming during a hands-on demonstration: "If this were real, you would have killed her! Oh my God, Sara, have you not been studying?" Deeply triggered, my brain slowly shut down as he rambled off all of the things I'd done wrong. Tears flooded my eyes as I wondered why the hell I was even there. And then I did what I needed to do. Taking a breath, I looked at the grass and paused. I reminded myself that my worthiness isn't attached to a pass or fail. I have already lived through some of life's most difficult traumas; saving someone is far more than knowing what to do in the outdoors. My inner critic tried to hijack my self-worth, but my heart said, *Go away. We've got this.* Wiping away tears, I pulled my instructor aside and explained why learning sometimes can be hard for me. I asked for kindness, patience, and a little understanding, and I promised to learn it all and pass. Which I did.

A crucial part of deepening self-worth is understanding your inner critic, the voice in your head that enjoys picking out everything you do wrong or poorly. He or she will judge your actions, thoughts, feelings, and worthiness. Early in my trauma healing, when I first started getting to know my inner critic, I imagined her as my devil-saboteur who sat on my shoulder, whispering all the things I wasn't supposed to be doing, couldn't do, or shouldn't attempt.

Sometimes our inner critic mimics those who have verbally hurt us, such as our parents, partners, or friends. My inner critic would even spew my former husband's stinging words: "You think you're so great, but you aren't. Get over yourself." He'd use these words to discredit, judge, or hurt me, mainly when drinking. Now I see that his words were projections from his own insecurities. This doesn't excuse his behavior, but understanding where these words originated helped me during my healing and forgiveness process.

Previously, when my inner critic spoke, I responded with fighting words. I'd close my eyes and get angry, pushing her off my shoulder into an imaginary deep abyss. Today, instead of anger, I lead with compassion and laughter. As my forgiveness for others and myself has taken hold, I no longer feel like fighting—not even with my inner critic. When she pops up, I take a moment to assess why she's there. *Am I tired? Do I need to get outdoors? Am I giving too much to others and not receiving enough myself?* And then I sit with my inner critic and politely say, "I see you. I hear you. And please leave. I am good."

When your inner critic interrogates your worthiness, judges

your actions, obstructs your goals, or sabotages your learning, you must remember to take a pause. The tendency to shift into fight, flight, or freeze mode when triggered is something you should be aware of. It's typical to want to fight or flee your inner critic, especially if you've experienced trauma.

To pay attention to the narrative in your head, you must stop in the moment, put your hands over your heart chakra, and take a breath. Slow your mind and sink into your heart. Ground yourself by sitting, or feel your feet touch the floor or earth under you. Notice where your energy is landing in your body and where your emotions are stemming from. Once your breath slows and your heart finds a natural rhythm, ask yourself these questions:

- Is my inner critic sharing accurate and true information?
- Is this information important for me to hear?
- Is my inner critic sabotaging my well-being?
- Is my inner critic speaking in my best interests?

If the narrative from your inner critic is unhelpful, unwarranted, or unnecessary, have a conversation and tell her or him to please leave. By not tolerating this type of behavior from your critic, you're teaching yourself and others how to treat you. Ultimately, you're feeding your self-worth and self-love.

Your Worthiness Is Not Dependent on a Relationship

If you have low self-esteem, it's common to turn to another human being for validation and love. However, love from another person cannot replace the love you have for yourself. I'll say it again: *the most important relationship you have is with yourself.* Being in a partnership or relationship with another human being is wonderful. But you should never allow your partner or relationship to define who you are in this world. Your love and self-worth don't come from being loved by your child, partner, parents, or friends. Love of self and worthiness both begin and end with your own heartbeat.

Let's go back to step two, when we discussed values. Ideally, you enter a healthy relationship with a person who has values similar to your own. Your hope is for the other person to continue living in alignment with these shared values. If the other person alters the balance and does not honor your values, the relationship becomes misaligned. When this happens, the partnership may crumble and break down. The same holds true for your worthiness and love for yourself. Both people in the relationship are responsible for working on their individual love for self, worthiness, and self-esteem. Of course you want your partner to validate his or her love for you, but if you continuously turn to the other person to feed your light, the relationship becomes off-balance, codependent, unequal, and unhealthy. Simply put, by loving ourselves first, we become better lovers.

Many of us have been hurt by past relationships with toxic codependency, when we relied on the other person for emotional and psychological support—including me. Having been married so young and for so long, I can now see when I began to lose myself in the relationship. I couldn't imagine living without this man I deeply loved. I would have given my life for him, not realizing that his struggles weren't my struggles. And his journey wasn't my journey. He needed to develop his own self-worth and self-love, not turning to me to feed his light, or to addictions to numb his pain.

Those of us who have experienced this type of relationship usually are determined never to allow this to happen again. To protect our hearts and souls from being hurt, we build barriers to keep us safe and create an independent existence. We need to recognize that we can balance independence and powerful partnerships. The best relationships value healthy intimacy, where deep personal development and growth also can be created.

To deepen your self-worth and self-love, you must better understand who you are. I'd like to guide you through two meditations with journal exercises. You will be taken on an honest, thought-provoking journey into your heart and soul.

In step two, you answered the question, "Who am I?" by uncovering values, connecting with your inner warrior, honoring wounds, and celebrating you. Now I'll guide you through two visualizations leading toward self-acceptance and forgiveness. After both visualizations, take time to journal your answers to the prompts. Sit cross-legged on the ground, and place both of your hands over your heart. If you cannot be outside, please sit on the floor or in a chair.

Guided Visualization to Better Understand Yourself

Close your eyes.
Take a deep breath in. And release.
Sink deeper into your body.
Notice where your energy flows.
Take another deep breath in. And release.

Slow your breathing and feel your heart.

Inhale for three . . . two . . . one. Exhale for three . . . two . . . one.

Now imagine yourself, alone, sitting in a calming forest. You are on a trail, surrounded by beautiful, towering pine trees. It's just you and Mother Earth.

Take in the view. Smell the fragrance of pine. Hear birds chirping in the distance.

Breathe in . . . three . . . two . . . one. Breathe out . . . three . . . two . . . one.

Embrace the beauty that surrounds you. The trees have been growing for hundreds of years and reach far into the sky above you. Notice as they dance with the wind in unison, their colors changing ever so slightly in each moment with the sunlight. This space has been created for this very moment. This space was created for you.

Feel the beating of your heart.

Two ravens appear, circling overhead. Seeing a raven signifies wisdom and intelligence. Ravens are a sign from nature that you have everything you need to figure out your next step. This is a reminder to pay attention to signs around you while sitting in the pause.

Breathe in . . . three . . . two . . . one. Breathe out . . . three . . . two . . . one.

You are alone with these beautiful birds. As you watch them glide freely through the air, you feel a sense of awe and wonder.

In this forest, you are free, without four walls confining

you. You no longer have responsibilities waiting for you. There's nothing around to distract you. You have no obligations. In this moment, you are at peace.

All you have to do is enjoy this incredible view. Everything you need to survive is in your pack: food, water, a first aid kit, a tent, a warm sleeping bag, and your favorite book.

Knowing this is all you have, how does this make you feel? What emotion comes up for you? Where does that emotion land in your body? Is there anything else you need, truly need, besides the items you have in your pack?

Take another breath in.

And as you breathe out, allow the exhale to ease any anxiety you might be feeling.

You are safe. You are good.

Suddenly, you notice a deer walking toward you. Feel the gentleness and peace it provides. A deer crossing your path reminds you to be compassionate and loving to yourself and others.

You feel your heart beating as you breathe in . . . and as you breathe out.

Be with your body.

Now remember your values from step two and ask yourself, *Who am I?* Looking into the eyes of the deer, you feel his calmness. He gets you. And he holds no judgment. As you answer the question "Who am I?" be honest with yourself.

Ask yourself:

What lights me up?

What can I release that no longer serves me?
What do I truly desire?
Keep your hands over your heart.
Breathe in . . . three . . . two . . . one. Breathe out . . .
    three . . . two . . . one.
The deer walks away, and you sit in silence.
Pay attention to the earth supporting you.
Smell the air. Feel the breeze. Let yourself smile. You are
    here. And you have everything you need.
Allow your body to come back to this time and space, and
    begin to bring gentle stretches to your fingers and toes.
Open your eyes and take a moment to look around.
Close to your heart, hold the things that make you who
    you are.

When you're ready, begin journaling the answers to the questions that were asked during the visualization, as well as a few additional questions to further your self-examination:

- What lights me up?
- What can I release that no longer serves me?
- What do I truly desire?
- How do I show up in this world today?
- How could I show up better in this world tomorrow?
- What are my barriers to achieving my goals and aspirations?

- Where do I find my enjoyment in life? And with whom?
- What are the gifts I bring to this world?
- What is my purpose and passion in life?

I encourage you to take your time when writing and revisit this visualization when you need to do so. We're always growing and learning. This visualization will guide you through better understanding yourself.

The next guided visualization is a second step in building self-worth and self-love. In this world, we're all deserving of being accepted for who we are. But first, we need to accept ourselves. That requires you to see your mistakes and patterns that no longer work. Then you let go of expectations and replace your self-criticism with compassion and forgiveness.

Guided Visualization to Invite Self-Acceptance and Forgiveness

Place your hands over your chest and feel your heartbeat.
Take in a deep breath. And release.
Feel the earth supporting you.
Continue taking deep breaths and allow your mind to calm. Slow your breath. Be here.
Now imagine you are walking beside a beautiful creek surrounded by long grass and brush. Take in the sounds around you and appreciate the beauty.
You see a pile of rocks stacked in the middle of the creek

and decide to take a seat. The feeling of refreshing,
cool water flowing around you is pure and calming.
Life seems simple in this peaceful moment.
There is no judgment. Notice this calm feeling.
Breathe in and breathe out. Feel your heartbeat.
Now imagine taking every worry, mistake, and judgment
you have been carrying and placing them in the water.
They wash away and are no longer yours.
Wrap your arms around yourself, embracing yourself in a big
hug. It's time to let go of the judgment and criticisms
and begin loving yourself for being you. Honor your
flaws and mistakes. They are part of you. Fully accept
that you are not meant to be perfect. No one is.
Now say these words out loud:
"I am loved.
I am worthy.
I embrace every part of me—those parts I love and those parts I
do not. Because I am me.
I forgive myself for any faults I have been carrying.
I will be fiercely compassionate to my heart, body, mind, soul,
and spirit!
I am needed and wanted in this world."
Take in a deep breath and release.
Feel the sun on your face.
You are loved in this moment and every moment that
follows because you know that love, value, and
worthiness begin with you. It doesn't matter how many
cars you have, the house you live in, or what material
items you own. What matters is who you are at your
core and how you treat yourself.

What a powerful choice and responsibility to have!

That is self-worth and self-love.

Breathe it in. And exhale it out.

Honor yourself and say, *"I love myself. I love myself. I love myself."*

Feel your heartbeat as you bring attention back to this time and place.

Breathe in. And exhale.

Come back to your body and slowly open your eyes.

Bring this self-love with you as you move into the rest of your day.

> When you're ready, set a timer for five minutes and free write about this experience. How did it make you feel? What realizations came up for you? After you finish, respond to these two prompts:
>
> List all of the things you love about yourself.
>
> Write about the things you once didn't love about yourself and now do. How can you better appreciate those parts of you?

Begin noticing your thought patterns in life and how you speak to yourself. When being self-critical, ask yourself, *Would I speak to another human being this way?* If the answer is no, then stop. You can change these behavior patterns, but first you must be aware of them. This is not only good for you—others watch how we treat ourselves and they, too, learn from our ways. Practicing self-love, worthiness, and fierce self-compassion invites forgiveness into your life.

EMBRACE SELF-WORTH + SELF-LOVE

In step four, we'll discuss how to set boundaries according to your values and from a place of love and worthiness. This is a needed step on your path to forgiveness. By setting boundaries with those who have hurt you, you prevent further damage. You validate your needs by saying, "I am worthy of setting a boundary that protects, loves, and honors who I am." I look forward to working through step four with you, one of my favorite steps.

Set Boundaries for Yourself

For most of my life, I was the people pleaser who cared about others before caring about me. I was the giver who listened when exhausted or helped when I knew it probably wasn't in my best interests. Many times this left me depleted, resentful, and at times, angry. Recently a woman said to me, "I'd love to go for a walk with you and share how my life relates to yours because you're such a nice person. I don't want anything from you. And of course, if you'd like to share your life with me, that would be fine too." Years ago I would have hung on to the words "you're such a nice person" and felt a responsibility to schedule the walk.

Instead, I knew—in this particular instance—that agreeing

to this wouldn't serve my needs or values. I graciously responded with, "Thank you, and though that sounds lovely, with limited time and energy, my primary focus is on my kids and projects." As a single mom of three sons, I have had to set aside my ego and desire to please everyone, and instead learn boundaries to take care of me. An important reminder: *we cannot take care of others without taking care of ourselves.*

I didn't realize how nonexistent boundaries were in my marriage until early in my trauma recovery. I remember hearing the term *boundary setting* and feeling ashamed that I didn't understand what that meant or how to use it in life. Perhaps it was my Midwest upbringing, the fact that I became a mom at such a young age, or that I was raised during a time when women's voices weren't heard as much as they are today. The concept of getting what I needed by telling someone else my rules of engagement felt hopeful and freeing, but also confusing because of my former way of thinking. But I also was at a point in my life when I knew something had to change. Giving of myself for so many years began to wreak havoc on my body, mind, and spirit. At what point do you say, "Enough is enough"? Realizing it was time to take care of me, I chose to surrender to a new way of living in this world and made boundary setting a top priority.

In step three, we talked about the importance of and how to achieve self-worth and self-love. In step four, we'll take action to create space for you, your thoughts, beliefs, needs, wants, and desires, by learning to set healthy boundaries. This is an incredibly important step on your road to healing and forgiveness. You are teaching others how to treat you on this healing journey, and you are learning what is good for your own heart, soul, body, mind, and spirit. I work on healing and forgiveness daily. And boundaries allow me to say, "This is good for me," and "This is not." Sometimes I overstep my own boundaries or don't hold them as firmly as I should. Today, I am aware when something doesn't feel right and I have to adjust a boundary. Boundary setting and maintaining is a continual work in progress. In this step you will:

- Understand what boundaries are—and are not. Healthy boundaries guide another person to know how you will, or will not, accept being treated. They create safety and security, and allow you to live a life in freedom, peace, and authenticity. Boundaries are necessary in every relationship, and you have every right to change or shift your boundary with another person.
- Learn how to set boundaries. I will share my five-part process to create healthy boundaries in life. Use this in your personal or professional life.
- Discover how one boundary can create many lessons. I had a client who accidentally dropped her phone over an embankment of the Grand Canyon. I will share the multitude of lessons that were learned when I had to set a hard boundary for safety reasons.

Please curl up beside your favorite tree or lie on the grass with your journal and book. Together, let's create space for your needs, wants, and desires using the one tool that has forever changed my life: boundaries.

/k

Clients often tell me some variety of the following: "I thought after my divorce I would close the door, walk out of the marriage, and move on. But it turns out I've only become more confused about who I am and what my needs are!" By walking out and closing the door on life's difficulties, without diving into and healing the pain, you feed darkness. It becomes the gremlin in life that grows behind the closed door. Many people come to me when the gremlin of their past life is too much to bear. For example, many would love to have a partnership but don't understand why all their relationships fail. Or perhaps, as parents, the relationship with their kids has faltered and they're evaluating the cause. Whether the trauma is from divorce, death, or any experience that shook up our lives, we cannot move into a healthy future without understanding our pasts and mending our hearts and souls. The process starts with us.

A question I ask my clients is: "Can you grow a tree on top of a stump?" Their reply is always no. Now imagine that your old life is the stump of a tree that has been cut down. The only way to grow a new life in its place is to dig up the tree and its roots, replanting a tree in soil you have prepared. Your life is no different. You cannot create a new future without taking care of what holds you in the present and past. Learning how to set boundaries will welcome new growth in your life.

I've had to do the same work. Through the discovery of my husband's infidelities, I was grieving not only the loss of him and our marriage but also the loss of the woman I knew I would never be again. Stepping into recovery meant looking at my life—past, present, and future—and learning to forgive myself along the way. The only way to walk through all of this was to understand how to set boundaries for me and others while I healed myself. I had to witness my past behavior patterns, understand how I got in this messy relationship, see where I needed to take responsibility, and identify the red flags so I never found myself in this same place again. Not everyone would appreciate or understand why I needed to put me first. But how they reacted to what I needed didn't matter. You should never apologize or feel bad for setting a boundary for yourself.

At first this process can seem difficult and hard. It's no different from traversing the Grand Canyon. My first hike was painful. I had stomach cramps, my legs hurt, and all I wanted to know was "Are we there yet?" But the more times I have hiked down and out of this magical space, the easier it has become. My body and mind take over and I never second-guess if I'm going to make it. Ultimately, you are in control of both your actions and reactions to everything in life, including this process of setting boundaries.

First, let's gain a better understanding of boundaries:

- Boundaries are for you. Boldly setting boundaries creates safety and self-love, and makes a statement that you matter.
- Boundaries teach people how to treat you, and by setting boundaries you're stating what you will and will not tolerate. Many times setting boundaries will also teach other people how best to treat themselves.
- Boundaries will make everyone "stay in their lane" and hold themselves responsible to fix their own problems, while learning important life lessons.
- Boundaries are the line in the sand that says, "If you cross this line, here is what will happen . . ." A boundary is only a boundary if you follow through on your end. We'll discuss more of that later in this step.

- Boundaries do not make you a villain or a mean human being. In fact, they do the opposite. Boundaries create freedom for you to live and express life in your way. Without boundaries, you're not stepping into your highest self and way of being in the world.

Let's use a client experience from the trail as an example throughout this step. It's the most powerful lesson of boundary setting I've had within the Grand Canyon. The learning was multifaceted, and it started with a woman accidentally dropping her phone down an embankment.

Having set out after breakfast to hike a few miles on the Clear Creek Trail, we stopped at a vista providing a view of Phantom Ranch below. It was a warm day, we had just completed most of the climb in elevation, and we were in good team spirits. Suddenly I heard a scream and all sorts of commotion. "Sara, we need help." I turned to find a client frantically wanting to reach her phone, which had dropped below her and was positioned by a small tree. She looked desperate. Others in our group held her back as she and I assessed the situation.

Sitting with my client on a rock, I calmed her down and asked her why the phone was so important. She told me about pictures she'd taken with her son that weren't backed up on iCloud or her computer. As a mother, I understood her need to retrieve the device, which to be fair, I easily could have done. But we weren't doing so while in a stressful situation. She became furious as I explained that her feelings were valid, but her safety came first. I could feel her resistance to the boundary I had set when she asked, "Can I please get it? Nothing is going to happen to me!" and I replied, "No."

"No" Is a Complete Sentence

You never have to explain yourself when setting a boundary that keeps you, your children, friends, family, or others safe. Period. If you feel you're at risk for harm, or if others' actions will cause harm, your needs take precedence over others' opinions.

In this chapter you will work through a five-part process for setting boundaries. Please use my response to my client to remind you that your *no* has every right to be used. If the person receiving the *no* ignores the boundary, take a step forward and regain your power to always put you and your voice first. If this client hadn't listened to my *no*, I had made eye contact with three men in my group, who were ready to step in and help regain control of the situation. You see, my boundary wasn't only for her—it was for all of us. When we set boundaries, others watch and learn. The way I used my tools to set the boundary with her showed others how their voice can be used outside of the canyon.

My client wasn't having it. What started as a phone holding her son's pictures turned into a battle of authority, both over ownership of the phone and wanting to prove who was right. Looking in my client's eyes, I thought, *Of course this would happen.* She was the same client who had shown up with resistance to being held, hugged (which I do a lot of), showered with love and laughter, and taken care of. Calming her with my touch, I said, "Hon, if there is any way to get the phone, I will. But not now with all of this commotion. You need to be okay with detaching from a device and walking away. Memories are held in the heart."

She looked at me and said, "You aren't letting me get it, are you?"

I replied, "Because I love and care about you, no."

Every boundary is held with love and compassion, regardless if the person receiving it is a kind human or a narcissistic energy vampire. You hold boundaries with positive energy in order to feed life's light, not darkness. Boundaries are stepping-stones to forgiveness, and forgiveness cannot be created from darkness.

As we continued hiking, I said to her, "I believe everything in life happens *for* us, not *to* us. I promise to think about ways to get the phone later. But for now, your opportunity is to see your anger, frustration, and resistance toward others caring for you. Let's work through the emotions, letting them go while also seeing the beauty around you. Be compassionate to yourself and forgive yourself for dropping the phone. This was an accident that could have turned deadly with carelessness. Detach from the phone and love your son for those experiences you had together. It's not about the pictures—it's about how you felt when you were with him. You have a choice in your reaction to this situation. When you walk out of this canyon, do you want to remember dropping your phone? Or the beauty and fun with these magnificent humans in this space? You choose, because eventually you will get a phone. Either your old one that is now behind you or a new one at home."

She asked to hike alone and be with her thoughts and feelings. I agreed and stepped away, watching as she moved through her emotions with each step. Being in nature gives the universe an opportunity to place our biggest lessons in front of us. We don't always like what is handed to us, but surrendering to the situation is key to accepting what's happening and letting the process unfold. Our own egos can easily interfere, as we want to force our opinions and what we want to see happen. But we will never "win" because the lesson will continue being handed to us until we choose to learn whatever it is we need to learn.

Looking back at my client, I saw her smile and knew she was shifting into acceptance of the boundary I had given her.

The Boundary-Setting Process

Let my client's story inspire you not only to set boundaries for others but to learn from setting them for yourself. It's equally important to understand that when people set boundaries for you, you have an opportunity to listen, learn, and grow into the boundary. Fighting what is there will only create more resistance.

Now I'll take you through a five-part process to establish healthy boundaries, which will create more space for your needs, wants, and desires in life.

Part One: Know Your Worth

We have worked on self-worth throughout this book, especially in step three. To maintain your boundaries with others, you must value yourself. The greater your love for yourself, the more firm you hold your boundaries and say, "Enough is enough." Which in turn feeds your self-worth and self-love, a beautiful cycle that can be hard for people when they've experienced much pain, betrayal, and loss.

When I stepped back and evaluated my dating life post-marriage, I realized how sick my own heart had been and what little self-worth I had. Dating can present challenges for a single, busy mom who hadn't been asked out in twenty years. With the encouragement of my boys, I made myself available in the dating world nearly two years after my marriage ended. My oldest son advised me to start asking men out, while my middle son hugged me after horrible dates and told me to have faith. My youngest only cared if the guy who took me out could play basketball. What I seemed to attract were men who weren't interested in long-term relationships and only sought casual sex and laissez-faire companionship. After all I'd been through, I knew this wasn't healthy for me. This confused me and caused a lot of chatter in my mind, heart, and soul. Early in my recovery, self-deprecating thoughts slammed my ego. I wanted so much more, but after living in a marriage with little intimacy, I was unsure how to find or receive what I knew I wanted. *Is it even possible from someone who has a bruised heart, soul, and ego?* The answer is a definite yes.

Of course, the mind loves playing tricks on the heart, and thus began the self-doubt and shame. *Am I even worthy of this if I can't seem to find it? Look at what I'm attracting! Maybe this is what I deserve and what my life has come to.* My ex-husband had good qualities, but as we know, he had rather big faults as well. When he fed his darkness and chose to lead a double life filled with betrayal, his demons came out to play. Sadly, I never knew the demons were in his presence. As a result, his behavior—the emotional abuse and manipulation—helped destroy my self-worth. I don't believe he was consciously trying to hurt me or make me feel less than. Even so, his actions fueled my belief that I'd never be enough.

Deepening my self-worth and setting hard boundaries in dating was as much for my kids as it was for me. They deserved a mom who allowed herself to receive and be in a healthy relationship. We want the best for our kids, and I know my kids want what's best for me. One night as I was crying in bed, curled up with my teddy bear, my middle son entered my room. He held me in his arms and said, "Mom, you will meet someone. You are incredible, and you have to believe that. I love you." At that moment, I chose to look at the love my kids, family, and friends feel for me, and refused to accept anything less from a partner. This is a boundary rooted in worthiness and love, which I hold firm in my dating life today.

Many professionals say it's damaging for children to hold their parents' pain. However, I believe it's a gift for children to see vulnerability from adults. Children should never feel responsible for fixing your pain or being the sole source of your love. But it's okay to sit in mutual love and respect for where you are at in this time in your life, showing worthiness for one another while understanding that we're human and all on our own journeys.

> Let's go back to step three, when I asked you to complete this sentence from your heart.
> My self-worth is honored when _____.

We stand in our worthiness by honoring our values. By holding the boundary of *no* with my client in the Grand Canyon, I honored her safety and life, our love for each other, the group dynamics, trust, and respect. The *no* fed everyone's self-worth and self-love.

I encourage you to find an item you can hold on to, wear, or look at when you need a worthiness reminder. I wear a diamond, heart-shaped necklace my parents gave me. When your boundaries are being tested and you're feeling forced to cave in to others' demands, touch or look at the reminder you choose and remember that you're setting boundaries to feed what is most important: *you*.

Part Two: Breathe and Protect Your Energy

Your energy is your force field. For people who have an innate desire to help or give to others, you tend to hand over your energy in the process, often feeling depleted and used afterward. Or you may be the type of person people cling to because your "light" or "good energy" is attractive. I think of it like the weather. People love sunshine and light winds that make them feel good. They're not drawn to hurricanes, cyclones, and rainy days.

When walking a path toward forgiveness, you must protect the most precious commodity you have: your energy. Setting energy boundaries with those you choose to forgive is a practice in self-love and self-worth. And it's not always easy. In my TEDx Manhattan Beach Talk, I shared the following: "I work on forgiving every day. It's sort of like a twelve-step program. I will be on this forgiveness journey for the rest of my life."[1] Caring for my energy has become a daily practice in my "twelve-step program." Those I have chosen to forgive, and continue to forgive, have drained me in the past. Therefore, I recognize the importance of separating myself from energy vampires or drama situations when needed.

Identifying the type of energy vampire you're protecting yourself from is also crucial. Dr. Judith Orloff, author of *Thriving as an Empath: 365 Days of Self-Care for Sensitive People*, shared the five most common types—the narcissist, the victim, the drama king or queen, the control freak and the critic, and the passive-aggressive—and how to block their ability to suck you dry.

1. THE NARCISSIST: "They're in it for the power over another person," Orloff said of narcissistic energy vampires. "If they can control you by, say, giving you the silent treatment or gaslighting you, that's a power play."[2] *Gaslighting* is a form of psychological manipulation "in which a person or entity, in order to gain more power, makes a victim question their reality."[3]

   To protect your energy, stay away from narcissists as best you can. The best way is to detach completely and cease all contact. Block them from your phone, social media, and any other communication. If that's impossible due to coparenting or other reasons, take control of what you can and limit interaction. Using the complete sentence "no" is healthy with narcissists. As Dr. Orloff stated, "Full-blown narcissists always see it as your problem. They can never own it."[4] Do not expect them to change.

2. THE VICTIM: "The victim, or the 'poor-me,' is somebody who doesn't take responsibility for themselves. The world is against them," Orloff explained.[5] Victims offer up every problem in their life, and when handed solutions, respond with reasons they won't work. I tell my clients that shifting from victim to survivor begins with you. Change the "Yeah, but . . ." to "Okay, and . . ."

   To protect your energy, do not be their therapist, coach, or doctor. Provide numbers for them to call while sharing how much you care, but it's their responsibility to fix their problems. In fact, by attempting to take on their issues, you're treating them like victims, enabling them and disallowing healing and growth.

   As a parent and former teacher, I believe that we model

healthy behaviors for our kids, and this is a great place to start. Many children take on a victim mentality and want parents or others to rescue them. When we do so, we aren't teaching our kids how to take care of themselves. They thus become dependent on outside sources to fix their problems. For kids to survive and thrive in the world and one day become healthy, independent adults, they must own their actions.

3. THE DRAMA KING OR QUEEN: Everything—and I mean everything—is a *big* deal in a drama king or queen's life. As Dr. Orloff stated, "This constant amplification demands an audience, and in turn, drains the audience's mental energy."[7]

   To protect your energy, try to not start a lengthy conversation with open-ended questions. Keep it short, sweet, and to the point. Dr. Orloff stated, "You can also set very clear, loving boundaries with them and say something like, 'You know, I'm on a big project right now, but I'm holding good thoughts for you. Just know I'm thinking of you.'"[7]

4. THE CONTROL FREAK AND THE CRITIC: The control freak tells you how to do everything, while the critic tells you everything that is wrong. This leaves you self-evaluating, confused, and wondering if you do anything right.

   To protect your energy, remind yourself that criticism seldom has anything to do with you. It's usually a projection of the other person's insecurities. "With the controller, you can say, 'Thanks for your input, I'll think about it,' and just keep moving. Don't get into it, and don't try and control a controller, as that seldom works," said Dr. Orloff.[8]

5. THE PASSIVE-AGGRESSIVE: They say one thing but do

another. Emotions and actions are rarely aligned. Passive-aggressive people will sabotage situations to gain control. Orloff said, "A passive-aggressive person is someone who expresses anger with a smile."[9]

To protect your energy, speak up and hold passive-aggressive people accountable for their actions. How they respond isn't your responsibility. But staying silent will cause anger, frustration, and resentment for the situation.

I'd love to share tools I use when I'm being confronted by or interacting with energy vampires. The first thing I do is imagine my body within a clear bubble that surrounds me. My energy only leaves when I give it permission. The bubble protects me from critical or condemning thoughts, actions, words, and dark energy. Everything thrown my way bounces off my force field and flies back in the direction it originated.

The second thing I do is call in my guardian angels, those who have gone before me, spirit guides, my inner warrior, and Mother Nature. In my mind or aloud, I say,

I'm calling in [who you choose],
    Please protect me (us) from dark energy and critical, condemning thoughts, words, and actions from others. Please bring love, understanding, and compassion to this moment. Allow your love and light to wash over the negative and darkness. Please keep me (us) safe.
    Thank you.

When we enter every situation in life with love and light, either for ourselves or others, darkness will never prevail. This is a choice and an expression of who we are. It's a way of being in this world—and it takes practice.

I used these tools when arguing with my client about her phone. I felt her hateful and angry energy rise, and I chose love by protecting me from her toxicity and calling in angels, spirits from the Grand Canyon, and my inner warrior to wash peace and light over the situation. Love will always win.

Part Three: Set Your Expectations and Agreements

An expectation is what you hope for or desire from the other person. However, the other person might not meet that expectation. It is not foolproof. For example, I can expect my ex-husband to continue therapy and recovery for the benefit of our children, but without having a conversation and setting a boundary, I only have my word. Having a healthy conversation and setting an agreement with a boundary require the other person's agreement. This shifts responsibility and creates more balance between the giver and the receiver.

My ex-husband relapsed over Labor Day 2015. My children and I were spending the weekend in Palm Springs at a basketball tournament while, to the best of my knowledge, he was working. Monday morning I woke to apologetic, scary, triggering, and cryptic text messages from him. I knew something was wrong. After attempting phone calls with no response, I woke my kids, took them to their final game, and began driving home. He finally called me, and hearing his voice, I knew he was tripping on drugs. I feared for his life. I called the police to check on him and decided I would no longer carry his addictions and unhealthy lifestyle in our lives. My kids asked, "Is Dad going to die?" Taking a pause, I responded, "I told you boys I would never lie to you because I know how badly it hurts when people don't tell me the truth. So I'll be honest. I don't know if Dad is going to die. But Mom is doing everything she can to get him help. Your dad needs to make the choice to be healthy, for himself and for us. I can't do that for him." They responded with silence. I said, "I love you guys," and looked at them in the rearview mirror. They said, "We love you too." The look in their eyes broke my heart.

Coming home and confronting my ex-husband took every bit of strength I had. I was devastated, disappointed, angry, overwhelmed with sadness, and I knew I was the only person who could protect our children from his dark behavior. No one, unless you've been in these shoes, can comprehend the overpowering feelings when you see someone you love hit rock bottom. You feel helpless. Yet you have to regain your power to create healthy boundaries. As hard as it is, it's the only way to keep everyone safe while in a difficult situation.

Forcing my ex-husband to look at me while I stood in the kitchen of his apartment, I said, "David, when you use drugs, drink, and live this toxic lifestyle, it hurts your children and me. It puts us at risk, and you too. I will no longer stand for it, and you will not see your children for two weeks unless you choose to get help. You may not talk with them in any way. No text messages, calls, or visits. You are not allowed around my home. When you choose to get help and show that you can live a healthy lifestyle, you may reengage with the kids and me. If you choose to die in a gutter, I will not hold the responsibility or shame. I only want what is best for you, but this is your choice, not mine." He responded, "I hear you, and I am sorry. I will do my best."

I followed through with no contact for two weeks. When

I knew it was safe, we did reengage, and our agreement holds true even today. I'm proud of him for hearing me and taking the steps needed to get help. That said, as with every addict, the choice is theirs on a daily basis. No one can or should do the work for them.

The script I used to hold the boundary with David was given to me by my coach and therapist, Dorit Reichental. This is a powerful tool to enforce your boundary. The person receiving the boundary may not agree, and that's okay. As Dorit taught me, "Boundaries are meant to be placed with love and are used for protection, but are not used to punish or to be punitive to the other person." Please alter this script to suit your needs:

- *When you* . . . (use drugs, drink, and live a toxic lifestyle)
- *It makes me feel* . . . (unsafe and not protected)
- *I will* . . . (no longer let you see or talk with the children or me)
- *Until you* . . . (seek the necessary help)
- *And when you come back to me and demonstrate that you understand the impact of the broken boundary, I will reengage and* . . . (you can be in our lives)

You can also see how, in the canyon, I used this script with my client. I explained to her that she was not allowed to retrieve the phone, while I also agreed to see if there were other ways to get it. In my mind, I knew I would attempt getting the phone on our way back when the group wasn't around me. To be clear, I wouldn't have agreed had I thought it unsafe or impossible.

Part Four: Detach from the Outcome

In step one of this book, I asked you to surrender to the outcome when setting your intention while on this journey toward forgiveness. Step four of boundary setting is much the same. Attaching to the outcome of a boundary holds you partially responsible for the result. However, you can only hold the boundary with another person, not force them to abide by your rules of engagement. Attempting to control how a boundary is received causes frustration, resentment, stress, and worry. It also doesn't hold the other person fully responsible for their actions.

Setting the boundary with my husband was hard, and I did it for his best interests. Yes, I did it for my kids too. But the primary person was him. Though my kids deserve a good father, we all need a healthy lifestyle. I had to surrender to his choice and outcome for recovery—otherwise I'd still be taking on his responsibility. Labor Day 2015 was the day I regained much of my power. I deepened my self-love, my self-worth, and my voice, and I taught my ex-husband that we all deserve respect.

Instead of focusing on and trying to control the outcome, which you ultimately have no control over, invest your energy in yourself. Spend time on self-care. Go for a walk and find five minutes of "soft fascination" in nature. Place your feet in the sand, ground yourself to Mother Earth, and breathe. Lean against a tree and recite the meditation from step one of this book.

When I feel anxiety creeping in, I know it's time for me to grab my stand-up paddleboard and hit the ocean for some calm and zen with dolphins and whales. I release the expectations and outcomes to Mother Nature and know I am fully supported. When journaling isn't an option, many times I use my phone to record my truths and emotions. That said, I'd like to share a journal prompt I hope you find helpful in shifting your energy:

> In choosing to detach from the outcome of this boundary, I am choosing to honor _____.

Part Five: Be Confident and Follow Through

A boundary only works if you're prepared to enforce it. If you set a boundary and fail to follow through, you're relinquishing control and agreements, as well as teaching the other person that your word doesn't matter. Accountability on your end is key. This can seem overwhelming and scary. But when following through with consequences, you're protecting your word, energy, safety, honor, and future. If the person you set the boundary with doesn't follow through on his or her end, you have every right to follow through on yours—without an "I'm sorry." In fact, by apologizing for taking necessary action, you dilute your power and the enforcement of the boundary itself.

I was fully prepared to follow through and enforce my boundary with my ex-husband. He would have given me no choice because he knew my rules for engagement and what I was willing to accept. Taking the step to follow through isn't easy, but you can do it.

Also remember that others are watching. Whether it's your kids, family, friends, coworkers, or society, when you begin setting boundaries with love, others notice and likely respect you more for it. Again, you teach people how to treat you. Not from a place of "I'm better than you," but from a choice to lead a healthy and drama-free life.

Boundaries Can Impart Powerful Lessons

Our time on Clear Creek Trail was spent sharing deep conversation, coaching, journaling, and meditating before hiking back to the main trail in two groups. As always, I was the last one walking off the plateau trail. I'm known as the "sweeper"— the last person who makes sure everyone is safely off the trail. Coming upon the vista where my client had dropped her phone, I stopped and saw how easy it would be for me to retrieve it. And so I did. Two other clients from my group knew what I'd done, and as we continued hiking, I asked them not to share this information.

I chose not to give the phone back to my client at that moment for a few reasons:

- She didn't need it.
- When she wanted to take pictures, others let her borrow their phones. What a great lesson in asking and receiving.
- I wanted her to work through the stubbornness she grasped on to when insisting on retrieving the phone. Surrendering to the situation has been a problem in her life, and what better time and opportunity to break the recurring theme?
- I saw her gradually lean in to and accept the phone's fate. I wasn't going to stop her process of letting go, a big lesson in her life.
- Trust is a value she was deeply working on. I told her I would make every attempt to get the phone, which I did. However, I waited for the perfect moment to hand it back.

We continued our day by hiking to Phantom Creek. Here we put on our water shoes and waded to a small waterfall. You could see the awe in everyone's eyes as they once again felt like kids. We took pictures of tadpoles and frogs. Noticed butterflies and heart-shaped rocks. We laughed, told jokes, and only cared about being in the moment.

Afterward, we started packing up and took a few final pictures. I called our group together and asked them to take a seat before hiking back to the ranch—there was something I wanted to share. Our day had been spent talking about values, boundaries, and self-love. Referring to when my client dropped her phone, I mentioned that I wasn't about to let anyone get hurt on the trail because I value others' safety. Looking up, I said to her, "I have something for you," and pulled out her phone. She leapt off the rock and ran to me in shock. I could sense her anger and happiness, and quite honestly, I expected her to express this anger. Instead, we hugged it out. I told her I loved her and that I could understand where she was coming from. I also asked that she understand my viewpoint, which she did. Knowing her day had hard moments of acceptance, she did a tremendous job working through the process. It was worth it when she said to me, "I don't trust easy. But you I trust. Thank you for teaching me it's possible."

If you take away any nugget of learning from this chapter, I'd love for it to be the message of *hope*. Boundaries are a work in progress, something we all continue to learn and lean in to. In our humanity, no one is perfect at setting or receiving them. Regardless of where you are in your life journey, you can trust that each and every one of us is always learning. With that, there is hope.

Now that we're well into our journey on the road to forgiveness, let's settle in during step five, as I share how to manage when the work gets hard. I'm proud of you for sticking with this process and allowing me to guide you through these steps. Freedom and peace are worth it—and so are you.

Persevere When the Work Becomes Hard

The first year after discovering my husband's double life was brutal. I was confused as to how my life came to this place. I felt abandoned and used. I was fighting for survival. My marriage was falling apart, yet I had to maintain a normal lifestyle for my kids.

Nearly eight months into recovery, our family took a planned trip to Montenegro with our son's water polo team for training. While there, and despite it having been a wonderful family adventure, I struggled with triggers that left me lost about the direction of our coparenting relationship. Such as the way our friends laughed with this man who was still my husband, but no one knew he was hiding a side of himself, and what he had done. It wasn't done with malice, but it hurt. I wanted nothing more than to keep my family together in whatever way possible, but at the same time, I felt pulled to run away and set myself free. Was it possible to ever release the anger and sadness? Could I sit without judgment and be in forgiveness? I wanted to, but it was hard when no one else knew the truth, leaving me to feel even more isolated and alone. Maybe he could handle living with secrets better than I could because he was used to it. I'm not sure. But living in this space felt wrong. My emotions ranged from sadness to happiness, love to hate, and anger to joy.

One afternoon, while hanging out at the beach with the water polo families, I was swimming in the Adriatic Sea when a parent said, "You look like you are beating the sh*t out of the water, Sara!" Though I can stand-up paddle from the mainland to islands, I don't swim well, which tends to surprise people.

And he was right. I *was* beating the crap out of the water. I laughed at his comment and thought, *Yeah, that's because I know how to fight to survive. Everything is hard right now.* Sometimes people say things without realizing the ramifications of their words. This was one of those times.

In step four, we learned how to set boundaries from a place of love and self-worth. So the question is: What can we do when the work gets hard? Do we lean in and fight, or let go and give up? This chapter will equip you with tools to guide you when you're ready to give up. I was there many times. My heart breaks when people say, "It was easy for you to work through your trauma. I don't get it." No, friends, it wasn't. In fact, I thought about suicide at age forty-one. This is an important topic for us to talk about. I'll share my experience and what kept me from going through with it. As I type these words, I think about my kids and am eternally grateful for my healing and life.

In this step you will:

- Learn about your comfort zone. Your comfort zone is the space that keeps you safe, and many times keeps you from living fully. By understanding what's holding you stuck and stagnant in your old ways and patterns, we can break those barriers and work through the challenging seasons.
- Go back to your intention. You need to remember why you're doing this work. With intention comes the reminder and clarity to continue moving forward.
- Set aside judgment and invite fierce self-compassion. I will guide you through a meditation to accept your hard moments not with judgment but with compassion and love.
- Raise your awareness about suicide. It's time to bring suicide into the light. Yes, you can be the person who wants to forgive someone who hurt you deeply while also being the person who wants to take your own life. The waves of emotions can paralyze you, moment by moment. Holding others' pain, as well as your own, can push anyone over the edge, including me. And what brought me into the light was understanding I had the power to forgive and let go of my pain. For those contemplating suicide, please read this section and know you aren't alone. There is hope, and your life has value.

Ih

I'd like to begin this step by sharing an insight. My ability to work through traumas never would have happened had I not become comfortable with stepping out of my comfort zone to face my fears. I'm writing this section while at The Sanctuary at Two Rivers in Costa Rica, attending a seven-day yoga retreat, something that is very unlike me. On a whim, I signed up for this retreat over six months ago. Yogis' abilities to slow their bodies and move with breath have always fascinated me, and to be honest, scared me. I know how to fight and do things well. But the thought of moving slowly, with intentional breathing, isn't something I'm accustomed to. Meditating on mountain summits, trails, or while on my stand-up paddleboard comes naturally. But moving on a mat does not.

Every year since 2013, I have signed up for things that scared me to my core—running ultramarathons, paddling to an island, hiking for seven days in the backcountry, starting a business, writing a book, or signing up for a yoga retreat. I knew that by achieving what I never thought possible, I was creating space for healing and overcoming my deepest traumas. Why? Because PTSD is scary, and with every barrier of fear I smashed, the stronger my heart, mind, and spirit became to face the betrayals and step into forgiveness. I think of it as the yin and yang in healing. As we face discomfort, we honor our strengths and bring our fears into the light, raising our deepest emotions and traumas into the presence of healing.

I knew that 2020 was the year to face yoga, something I've looked at from the outside for years. When I signed up for this retreat, I didn't realize I'd have a manuscript due at the same time. The resistance to board the plane was so powerful, my body couldn't make it to a yoga class before I left. So the morning of my flight, I flipped open my computer and followed along with a thirty-minute YouTube video. Emotions flooded me while lying on the carpet, and I cried before closing my computer and packing my bag. It was time, once again, to step out of my comfort zone and continue healing.

Clients will often say, "I was scared to sign up for your retreat. But I'm so glad I did. My time in the canyon was one of the most pivotal experiences in my healing journey."

Standing at the rim on the South Kaibab Trail, I feel into my clients' energy and body language while deciding who will lead. Unfortunately, many people don't view themselves as leaders—from moms and dads to caregivers and even CEOs. We have a thought of what a leader "should" look like, and sometimes we only think of ourselves as leaders in certain situations. In reality, we all have a leader within us, who's willing to guide us, with intention and forethought, through every personal and professional moment in our life. Knowing this, I intentionally pick a nervous and scared client to guide us on the trail. While this may seem mean or unfair, everyone in the group learns and grows through the leader's experience of facing fear while we support each step.

Please grab your journal and let's discuss your comfort zone. This is a necessary step to understanding what you are ready to face and learn.

What Is Your Comfort Zone?

Your comfort zone is the area of your life where you spend much of your time. I think of it as being an invisible circle that surrounds you, filled with things you do every day. You don't question "if I can" or even "if I should." When living in your comfort zone, you don't live in fear. Instead, you live in a place of safety and routine.

Athletes may have comfort zones filled with activities such as running, competing, and being a leader. Doctors' comfort zones may be filled with having difficult conversations, speaking, or performing surgery. Everyone's comfort zones are different.

The problem is that many times, especially in toxic lifestyles, you become comfortable with the uncomfortable. You don't know how to say no to people. Or you may not have the courage to step outside of a bad relationship you know isn't good for you.

You might need to seek help for addictions, leave a career that isn't right for you, or move from a place where you're unhappy. Even when you know a healthier way of life is at your fingertips, breaking free can be hard because "you don't know what you don't know."

I talked about "trauma bonding" in the preface, and how I stayed in my relationship because I was continuously drawn back to my husband's manipulative actions, which ultimately created a codependent and unhealthy way of life. To leave would have been hard, even though an easier lifestyle eventually would be found on the other side of the hard. I, too, suffered from mental and emotional abuse that left me feeling fearful, stagnant, and comfortable in an otherwise unhealthy and uncomfortable situation.

We all need to be able to step outside of our comfort zones in order to free ourselves from abuse and find healthy relationships, lean in to recovery from our past experiences, try new things, embrace forgiveness, and ultimately live life by our values. We deserve an opportunity to learn what we are truly capable of.

How Do You Grow Your Comfort Zone?

I'm going to teach you a process I use daily. It keeps me aligned in my values, allows me to look at the barriers before me, has supported me to step into forgiveness, and gives me the tools to live my adventurous life today.

- **LIST EVERYTHING YOU WOULD LOVE TO ACHIEVE IN LIFE AND AREN'T ACTING ON.** Don't think about whether it's possible to do these things or not. Simply list all of the things you'd like to do. I encourage my clients to do this from their heart and not their head. Remember, these are just things you'd like to consider doing.

  Some of my examples are:
  —moving to Costa Rica
  —traveling the world for a year
  —being in a committed relationship

  It's probably fair to say the items you listed are currently outside of your comfort zone, which is why you haven't taken action. What I would like to do next is help you understand what's holding you back from achieving these things.

- **LIST EVERYTHING HOLDING YOU BACK FROM ACTING ON WHAT YOU'D LIKE TO ACHIEVE.** Perhaps it's lack of funds or you don't have the confidence yet. What's preventing you from living your best life? I refer to these as your *barriers*, otherwise known as obstacles.

  We all tend to use barriers as reasons not to do something, which holds us back from living our deepest desires and dreams. However, we have the power to do what we choose. Sometimes we must seek help or guidance, or view the possibilities from a different perspective.

Some of my barriers to living in Costa Rica, traveling the world, or being in a committed relationship are:

—raising my boys

—lack of time

—not prioritizing

Before I started this work, I would have used my barriers as excuses for not achieving what I desire in life. For example, I would have said, "There is no way I can move to Costa Rica or travel the world. I have responsibilities and kids! What kind of mom would I be if I did that?" Today, I view life very differently. While raising my boys through middle and high school, I'm planning where I'd like to live after they graduate. I have an opportunity to invest in a future lifestyle that will benefit them as well. Perhaps I'll buy a place in Costa Rica, where they can visit and maybe someday bring my grandkids. I'm doing a lot of interpersonal work on my self-worth in order to receive a committed relationship. And I'm exploring the idea of traveling the world when I turn fifty years old.

In your journal, list the barriers holding you back from putting your yes into action. Anything's possible when you realize your barriers are nothing more than excuses and limiting beliefs holding you back from living your best life.

So how do you smash these barriers?

- **REFRAME THE STORY IN YOUR HEAD BY LOOKING AT YOUR BARRIERS AND ALIGNING WITH YOUR VALUES.** In step two, you worked on your values—your beliefs of who you are as a human being and the building blocks of your heart, mind, soul, and spirit. Your values become the basis of all resonant choices in your life. It's time to look at something outside your comfort zone and bring it into your life.

In your journal, take a moment to complete this sentence:
I am ready to say yes to _____.

As you learned, you have remained in your comfort zone because of the stories you have fed yourself for so many years. By standing in fear and doubt while telling yourself over and over why you can't do something, you're telling yourself that you aren't worthy or good enough to act on—much less try—the thing you want most. The more you tell yourself that story, the more comfortable it becomes.

A study in 1960 by Eleanor J. Gibson and Richard D. Walk showed we are "born with only two innate fears: the fear of falling and the fear of loud sounds."[1] Most fear is learned and used as a survival mechanism. However, when fear hinders us, we aren't standing in our values but rather diminishing the core of who we are. Knowing this, remember that you're the only person standing in the way of your yes. Growth begins outside your comfort zone.

To smash the barriers standing *before you*, you need to reframe the thoughts and stories *living within you*. For example, I told myself this story: *I can't go through a divorce and become a single mom. How can I lose my home, life, and family? Perhaps it's best to stay in this lifestyle until my kids are out of school.* But I reframed this story: *I have a voice, a life that matters, and my kids need a healthy mom. I wouldn't want them to live like this, so why should I be expected to? They*

111

deserve a strong family foundation, and I can create that, even if alone. At that moment, I replaced unworthiness and fear with my values of truth, hope, family, love, and connection with others. I can't imagine what my life would be like if I didn't do this work for me and my boys. As a result, I was able to have tough conversations, get a divorce, sell my home and nearly all of my belongings, and welcome a life led by choice. And most importantly, I was brave enough to forgive all of those people in life who hurt me the most, setting boundaries along the way. Through this process, I not only fed my values but also found my purpose in helping others.

Let's do the same for you!

Picture yourself standing on a mountain summit. You have been looking west, seeing your barriers from a place of self-deprecating thoughts. These thoughts tell you why you can't do something. The stories in your head saying, *You don't know how* or *What's the use?*

Now do a 180-degree turn and look east from a new place, facing your barriers from your values, the foundation of who you are. In place of telling yourself why you can't do something, reframe your reasoning to feed your values. Tell yourself, *I can do this, and here is how.*

> Once again, write in your journal and finish this statement.
> My barrier is _____. I will smash my barrier by _____.

Let me give you another personal example. To step into forgiveness with my husband, I had to step outside my comfort zone and confront mutual friends he had intimate relationships with during our marriage. My intention was to free myself and hand back the pain, anger, and sadness they'd put on me. You'll learn more about how to do this in step seven.

I was terrified. Before confronting them, I answered the question above with: *My barrier is my fear. I will smash my barrier by preparing myself before approaching the person my husband had an affair with. When I arrive at their home, I will put on my running shoes, then breathe and count to three before I get out of the car, run to the house, and knock on their door. I will have my script ready, speak my truth, hand back my pain, and grant forgiveness.* This is exactly what I did, step by step. And it worked. By facing my husband's lovers, I was valuing my self-worth, self-love, forgiveness of self and others, respect, integrity, truth, my life, my kids' lives, family, and hope, among many other things.

What values are you honoring by choosing to smash your barriers? Write these in your journal.

I encourage you to use this exercise for every yes you want to bring into your life. I still use it! If a red flag appears or you feel a flutter of self-doubt, take notice. Is it a story in your head fed by years of self-deprecating thoughts? Or is it something worthy of examining? Sit with your hesitancies and remember that you hold the power to rewrite your thoughts *and* your stories. There is a way and an answer. It may not always be one you want to hear or face, but *there is a way and an answer.* And if fear begins to creep into your mind, slow down, take a deep breath, put your hands over your heart, release your breath, and ground yourself to the earth. As I mentioned in step two, many times we misinterpret excitement as fear. Close your eyes and take a pause. Allow yourself to experience the emotion and discern whether you're feeling fear or excitement. Please question yourself. In doing so, you'll find your answers lie within you.

Go Back to Your Intention

When anything in life becomes hard, it's important to remember why you're doing this work. What are you working toward? As I said in step one, intention setting is important because you cannot make resonant, life-changing steps without having a clear understanding of what you're hoping to find.

That said, sometimes our intentions do change. I would like you to go back to step one, when I led you through a guided meditation for setting intentions, and remind yourself of what you found. What was it?

My intention for this journey is _____.

If you need to go back and read or listen to the guided meditation again, please do so. Often my intentions change several times when on a healing journey or on a trail. As the energy within you moves, your intentions also may shift.

As you learned in step one, there are four important things to remember when setting your intention:

- Keep your intention honest.
- Surrender your attachment to your outcome. Allow your intention to evolve.
- Keep your intention positive.
- Feel into your intention and the emotions that arise along the way.

When on my retreats, I frequently ask clients to check in with their intention every morning and evening, and when it gets hard on the trail. Because they release so much emotionally, mentally, and physically while hiking, they need to consistently check in with their hearts, minds, bodies, and souls. It's here, when outside their comfort zones and in nature, that they realize what they're capable of.

In the beginning of this step, I shared how I choose the person to guide us on our first steps into the Grand Canyon. I look for the person who is afraid, perhaps isn't used to being in such a leadership role, and exhibits a little anxiety. On one of my retreats, that person was Stefanie. (For privacy reasons, I have changed her name.) She came to me for help in getting out of her toxic and abusive marriage to a narcissist, which I did, and am so grateful to have been asked to do. Post divorce, she chose to go on a retreat as a step in her healing and growth. Stefanie was still dealing with effects from many years of mental, emotional, spiritual, and physical abuse. She was nervous about trusting the group members and had difficulty sharing. She said her intention for the retreat was "to be able to trust again." To trust others, we need to find trust within ourselves. For many reasons, including her intention, I had Stefanie lead us into the canyon. I wanted Stefanie to see the leader that we all saw within her. Throughout the retreat, when she began to go inward and not want to share or join us, my coleader and I would ask, "Have you done anything so far to show that you cannot trust yourself? Have we done anything to show that you cannot trust us?" The answer was always a definite no. By continuously returning to her intention, she left the canyon trusting again—both herself and ten other people. And without even being asked, she led us out of the Grand Canyon in the darkness of night, one foot in front of the other.

When you feel like you cannot take one more step in this work, go back to your intention. Recite your intention while walking in nature, putting your feet in the sand, hugging a tree, and breathing fresh air. Slow your mind; inhale and exhale. You are worthy of happiness, joy, love, peace, and freedom.

Release Judgment and Invite Fierce Self-Compassion

I've discussed judgment throughout this book. I find it's a conversation worthy of having on a daily basis. Judgment, I feel, has become out of control in society. We judge ourselves for never being or doing enough. We judge others for their religion, race, sexuality, what they eat, how they dress—the list goes on and on. At the core, however, we're all human beings with a heart that feels, a mind that thinks, a soul that speaks, and a body that moves. I didn't ask to be me any more than others have asked to be who they are. I will go so far as to say that in my past, because of what I'd lived through, I wanted to be anyone other than who I was. I, too, have felt the wrath of judgment. Whether it was as a seventeen-year-old girl who was called a slut because I was pretty and pregnant, or as a woman at forty-one who has heard many times, "I thought you were in an arranged marriage for his money." It's taken me a long time to heal from the judgment, and fully love and honor myself.

We must learn to take a pause and view others with understanding before making false assumptions. Knowing that judgment stems from a place of projecting one's own pain, I make a conscious choice to see the other person with compassion, empathy, and love. Pain triggers pain and hate breeds hate. I refuse to add more of either into this world.

Of course, we do need some judgment in our world. For instance, when I'm guiding clients on the trail, I take note of and judge their energy and safety, and where they are spiritually, emotionally, and mentally. I judge the weather and my group's ability to handle heat, cold, and any other environmental circumstances. Judgment can be a positive and helpful tool to keep us safe and secure.

Judgment becomes harmful to us and society when we don't give ourselves the opportunity to find forgiveness, acceptance, and understanding from our past experiences. When triggered in the present, we bring forth our emotions and feelings caused by our past pain. Many times this pain is generational, handed to us by our parents, grandparents, great-grandparents, and so on. This can create stories in our heads, false thinking, and even manifest hate, discrimination, and anger.

Let me give you an example. Recently a male acquaintance of mine, who works in the entertainment industry, posted a tweet stating that a female in the service industry had mistreated him. I happen to be friends with the female he accused of mistreatment. As someone who didn't witness the events and therefore cannot pass judgment, yet who knows both people, I read the tweet and was shocked not only by what was said but also by what manifested from one social media post. My heart broke because of the amount of anger, judgment, hate, vitriolic comments, and toxic emotions shared in thousands of comments against my friend. I felt compassion for my male acquaintance and his past experiences, which led him to write what he did. I felt sad for my friend, who never meant harm and is such a beautiful soul. And

I felt empathy for the thousands of people who quickly passed judgment on a woman they didn't know and a situation they weren't a part of. It's a reminder that what we say, whether good or bad, intentional or not, can create a wave of positive or negative energy in this world. Can you imagine if we approached all disagreements with healthy dialogue instead of arguing and hate-filled speech? We all have an obligation to take a breath before judging others—or ourselves.

We aren't provided a handbook or pamphlet on how to get through hard times in life. Though it would be nice if we were! To set aside self-judgment, invite compassion in and appreciate how far you've come rather than noticing how far you have to go. Stay present and be reminded that no journey is perfect. You're doing what you can with every day of your life, and personal development work never ends. Inviting forgiveness to your life is a practice. Some days the work is harder than others and you experience setbacks. Other days it feels like a breeze. Find a way to keep doing these steps and work through the process. Don't stop feeling your emotions or feeding the light within you.

Mindfulness

I would like to discuss the concept of mindfulness before I guide you through a meditation. Mindfulness is the practice of maintaining a moment-by-moment, nonjudgmental state of awareness for our thoughts, actions, and experiences.[2] When living mindfully, we're reminded that we have a choice in how we react to everything. For example, when you feel like giving up, or when you want to stop traveling the road toward forgiveness, you can view these thoughts and emotions for what they are, without judgment. Mindfulness lowers stress, blood pressure, and anxiety, and welcomes relaxation, clarity, and love.[3] We use mindfulness nearly every moment on the trail, noticing prickly pear cacti, the way sunrays shine through clouds, and how the colors of the canyon change with every passing hour. In step six, I'll share how being engaged in nature leads to mindfulness and can help with issues like depression.

I'd like to guide you through a short meditation for releasing judgment. I use this practice when anxiety creeps in, or when I feel overridden with triggers and negative thoughts. Have your journal and pen sitting beside you for a journal exercise after the meditation.

Guided Meditation for Releasing Judgment

Place your hands over your heart and take a deep breath in.
Hold your breath, and release.
Ground yourself to the earth.
Take another breath in and imagine your breath is coming
  from Mother Earth.
We are all connected.
We are one.
Allow her love to flow through your body, starting with
  your feet. Moving up through your legs. Into your
  stomach, chest, through your arms, hands, fingertips,
  and all the way up through your head.
Mother Earth's love is in you.

Release your breath.

Feel your heartbeat.

Now I will ask you, What are you judging?

Is it your fear? Your thoughts? Your anger or yourself?

What are you judging?

Release your hands from your heart and cup them in front
 of you.

Now imagine that you're tenderly holding what you are
 judging, bringing it into the light.

Take another breath in. And release.

Keeping your eyes closed, take notice of what you are
 holding.

Just sit with it.

Breathe in. And release.

Breathe in. And release.

As if you're setting free a bird, allow your hands to set free
 what you have been holding on to.

While doing so, recite this mantra with me three times:

I release my judgment and attachment to what I have been holding.

I release my judgment and attachment to what I have been holding.

I release my judgment and attachment to what I have been holding.

Breathe in. And release.

Bringing your hands back to your heart, continue grounding
 yourself to the earth. Feel the support under you.

You are safe.

You are safe.

You are safe.

Lifting your head to the sky, recite this mantra three times
 while imagining love from Mother Earth and nature
 flowing over you like a waterfall:

I invite self-compassion and love.
I invite self-compassion and love.
I invite self-compassion and love.
Take notice of your body and your breath.
Breathe in. And release.
The only moment that matters is the one you are in right now. Without judgment or fear, allow yourself to slow your mind and breath.
One more time, recite these words:

I release my judgment and attachment to what I have been holding.
I invite self-compassion and love.

My friend, you are enough.
You are worthy.
You matter.
You have everything you need to continue this road to forgiveness, peace, and freedom.
Feel your heartbeat. That is your heartbeat.
Breathe in this experience one last time.
Slowly opening your eyes, begin to come back to the here and now. Wiggle your fingers and toes.
Just be.

When you're ready, pick up your journal and complete this sentence:
By releasing judgment and choosing self-compassion and love, I am welcoming _____ into my life.

I use this exercise when triggered with emotions; when I feel overwhelmed as a mom, businesswoman, or friend; or when anxiety takes over. This tool can be used in the moment to realign your values, love, compassion, direction, and spirit.

Your Life Has Value

We cannot pass over the topic of suicide when discussing personal development work, healing, and traveling the road to forgiveness. Many times on my own journey I hit rock bottom and searched for hope.

According to new data from the research company YouGov, nearly one-third of Americans say they know someone who has committed suicide.[4] Until I personally felt the wrath of mental health issues, I couldn't understand how someone could take their own life.

When I lost my friend Heather to suicide many years ago, I remember hearing people talk about how those who commit suicide are "selfish." To this day, I cringe when I hear "selfish" and "suicide" in the same sentence. Battling internal demons or ruminating negative thoughts oftentimes leads to hopelessness and a feeling of despair. We'll never know what it's like to live in another person's altered state of mind. But from my personal experience, I know how horrible it is to struggle with mental health.

Heather didn't live in my mind and I didn't live in hers. What we all can do is speak up, offer a hand, and make others aware there is no shame in seeking help. As a society, we need to prioritize mental health and provide accessible programs, without judgment.

Let's start the conversation here and shift our awareness to mental health itself. We need to spotlight the misunderstanding, judgment, lack of funding, and shame we burden ourselves and others with when we're struggling with depression, addictions, anxiety, PTSD, and other issues. Since going public with my story, I've had hundreds of people message me and tell me they thought of taking their own life. The first thing I want to tell you is this: *you are loved.* I wrote this book for each and every one of you. Someone in Europe may be reading the same words as someone in Africa, or Costa Rica, or the United States. That I deliberately worked and manifested to get my story out there, and in this way, is proof enough that you are cared about. In fact, if I could hug all of you at this very moment, I would. But since I can't, please close your eyes and imagine that I am.

I believe we're all connected to one another, to nature, the universe, God, or whatever you may believe in. Yet, even with connection, we don't realize how many people around us have thought about ending their lives. As mentioned earlier, it's possible to want to love and forgive someone or yourself while also wanting to end your pain. Emotions are strong and can hold you in a state of depression, fear, anxiety, or unrest. You may not know what your next step is in life. For the longest time, my only next step was to get out of bed, take care of my kids, and immerse myself in nature on a daily basis. I gave myself permission to feel emotions without judgment while reminding myself that I didn't need answers to my life's biggest questions. *How will I make it? What will I do? Why did this happen? Can I ever end this cycle?* No one but me had been putting pressure on the unknown. And that is the reason I began step one with asking you to take pressure off of your choices in life.

I found hope in realizing that since it took forty years to get me to that moment, answers couldn't be unveiled in a day. I needed to release total control of the outcome and take healthy steps for me and my kids. One powerful, healthy step every day. That was the only expectation and agreement I had with myself.

For me, that meant trying to eat healthy and not drink to numb my pain. It took me a while to admit my family history with alcoholism, and once I did, I could see my own patterns with wine. I have never been one to take over-the-counter drugs, prescriptions, or illegal drugs. As I've said, meditating, mindfulness, going into nature, and exercise became a daily practice. I found a wonderful coach and therapist, and I joined a support group. Slowly, I regained my confidence, courage, and self-love, and eventually found the power to forgive and let go of my pain.

When the time was right and I was well on my healing journey, I shared with my boys how painful life had been in the past, and that I had thought about driving my car into the overpass on I-405 in Los Angeles. I wanted them to know how deep my anxiety and depression had been at times. I felt it important for them to understand how I couldn't eat or sleep, that I knew when their dad was relapsing, and how painful it was for me to let go of his responsibility. They needed to know that it's common to feel alone on an island without anyone to turn to, but I was proof you're never really alone.

By bringing my own shame and guilt into the light, I normalized mental health struggles, which is what we need to do as a society. The statistics are staggering. A study in the journal *Depression & Anxiety* found that in a sample of 1,433 subjects with recurrent early-onset major depressive disorder, 28 percent had attempted suicide, and PTSD increased the risk for

attempted suicide.[5] And a study published in *Psychiatry and Psychiatric Epidemiology* found th 94 individuals with chronic PTSD, more than suicidal thoughts, and nearly 10 percent had su after the trauma.[6]

The reason I didn't turn to suicide was because sons. They had already lost their family as they knew i essentially wasn't who they thought he was, and they h their way within that relationship. The thought of then abandoned by the one person who has never lied to or b them was too much for me to bear. And in spite of my hard I have always loved living. I decided I wasn't having that from me because of someone else's actions.

I wanted my kids—just as I want you, the reader— understand that none of us is alone, and there is no shan when we have mental health struggles. We're all affected by i at some time in our lives, and when we are, help is available.

If you or someone you know is thinking about suicide, please seek help from a professional or call your local suicide prevention line. The National Suicide Prevention Lifeline (https://suicidepreventionlifeline.org or 1-800-273-TALK [8255]) is a United States–based suicide prevention network with a toll-free, 24/7 hotline available to anyone in suicidal crisis or emotional distress. Help is only a phone call away.

Now that we've covered what to do when the work gets hard, let's move into step six, where we'll discuss the balance between "doing" and "being." I'll share client experiences from the trail that will leave you in awe. I look forward to continuing this road to forgiveness with you. Only two steps remain—I'm proud of you for staying the course!

STEP SIX
Do Less + Be More

While on personal hiking trips, I live in what I call the "flow." I have a destination in mind, but I keep a loose itinerary that allows me to stay present and open to whatever comes my way. I've hiked side trails I never knew existed, summited mountains I didn't know were passable, and shared camp with strangers who've become lifelong friends. Possibilities are endless when I discard unnecessary expectations, and choices turn into enjoyable learning experiences.

This practice is also how I live my life. Though I have goals for the future, I don't focus solely on where I'll be in ten years, much less two. It's about listening within as well as around me, and trusting that my life journey is unfolding as it's meant to at any given moment. This concept can be easy to embrace when all is well. But when difficulties arise, we tend to resist this thought process, as I did when I was recovering from the trauma of my marriage. My future felt on hold, and I wasn't okay with that. I wanted all of the answers and to know where I was headed. However, being in nature has taught me a valuable lesson: *by trying to control what is beyond our control, we deny ourselves happiness along the way.*

I learned a firsthand lesson in "flow versus control" on a Grand Canyon trip with a large group of friends. We planned to drive a van from the South Rim to the North Rim, where we'd stay overnight before hiking down and spending a few days in the canyon. This was six months after I discovered my husband's infidelity, and I needed to be alone on the trail. Instead of joining the group, I chose to through-hike from the South Rim to the North Rim, a twenty-four-mile trek. My intention was to see how fast I could complete this mission while finding joy in my happy place.

After I had shared my itinerary at dinner the night before, one of the guys said, "How about if I go with you?" I love hiking with this guy, but alarms went off inside me when he said those words. My heart sank and was telling me no, but my head felt it would be mean and selfish not to say yes. I knew he was interested in the trail I was taking, and he also wanted to make sure I was safe, which was kind of him. Reluctantly I said, "Yeah, sure. That would be fun." This experience would teach me the importance of listening to your intuition, speaking up for your needs, and the value of patience.

Early the next morning we set out on the trail. Calculating our distance after a few hours, I realized we wouldn't finish before dark. I was frustrated that my day wasn't turning out as anticipated. I'd hoped to reach the North Rim and watch the sunset with a cold beer in hand, and now that was impossible. By the time we hit the bottom of the Grand Canyon, my friend was exhausted and mentally drained, and didn't want to continue, but we still had another fourteen miles to get to the North Rim. I sat with him and wondered what to do. He said, "I'll be okay. You can go ahead and I'll take my time getting there." That would have been easier, taking off and exploring the last fourteen miles at my own pace. But I knew it wasn't right or safe. Taking a few minutes to myself, I walked around and asked for guidance from the universe. The response was loud and clear in my mind: *You cannot do anything but allow the remainder of this day to unfold as it's meant to. If you get out at 10:00 p.m., so be it. You have everything you need. This is your lesson in patience.*

I could have been angry with myself for not saying no in the first place, or at my friend for not being prepared enough. Yet there we were, stuck, and I was being pulled to surrender attachment to my emotions and blame. Taking a deep breath, I released expectations, anger, annoyance, and resentment. By accepting what was, I felt peace. Walking over to my friend, I smiled and said, "Hey, it's okay. Let's go slow and see what happens. I'm not leaving you."

It was a long, hard hike up the north side of the canyon that day. Though frustrating at times, I honor my friend's determination and appreciate the laughter and time spent sharing life stories on the trail. When anxiety and irritation arose, I used "I am patient" as my mantra to find beauty and gratitude in the moment. By surrendering control and allowing the world to be beside me—and me with the world—I learned a deeper understanding of and value for patience.

We arrived at our destination after 10:00 p.m. On the way, I helped struggling hikers out of the canyon, providing water, food, and light in the darkness. We also set up an emergency camp for a couple suffering from dehydration. I didn't just receive a lesson in patience. With our day unfolding as it did, we helped a lot of people too. Sometimes you don't know why things are happening until you view situations with an open heart instead of through a frustrated lens.

Living is what happens when you strive to *do less* and *be more*. By learning how to flow with your days, you don't waste your finite energy by forcing anything. Out of all the steps to forgiveness, this one has been the most difficult for me to embrace, which is why I made it step six.

Take your time with this step and try not to get frustrated. If or when you do, remember my moment at the bottom of the Grand Canyon and seek patience.

In this step, you will:

- Learn the difference between doing and being. There's a balance between setting life in motion while also allowing life to happen. We'll explore what's possible when you stop feeling the need to fix everything in life and instead simply be with your emotions and experiences. You cannot step into forgiveness without first feeling and honoring the anger, sadness, and resentment.
- Let go of the heavy, unwanted things you're carrying in life. Much of what we carry in life isn't even ours to hold, whether pain from others, responsibilities that don't belong to us, or ideas we disagree with. When you let go of everything that doesn't serve your highest good, you change

your thought process and how you show up in this world. I will walk you through the same powerful analogy I share with clients.

- Stop fighting and stop overcomplicating life. If I were to ask, "Is fighting fun for you?" I doubt you'd say yes. Fighting is toxic and requires a lot of your energy. By simplifying your life, you open yourself to bountiful ease, happiness, and joy.

I struggled to understand and implement the premise of this step when I was first introduced to it in my late thirties. Sitting still and using a form of quiet meditation in nature was something I did well as a child. In fact, I mentioned that earlier in the book. But through family patterns, years of schooling, and parenting, it became ingrained to celebrate when I crossed a task off my to-do list. The thought of stopping what I was doing and being quiet to listen seemed crazy. How could *being still* be more useful than *getting life done*? No one could convince me of this.

In many ways, my stubborn tendency to move fast through life prevented me from acting on red flags in my marriage. And, sad to say, through the plight and chaos of trying to fix my home life, husband, or whatever else was broken, I lost sight of myself. My busy life had taken over, and I couldn't sit still. I didn't realize what I needed most was exactly what I resisted.

How can you hear your wisdom and clarity if you're never quiet? My hope is to bring the same understanding to you that was offered to me: *you must slow down your body and mind, align with your heart and soul, and listen.* Being out of alignment is like trying to travel north with a compass that points northeast. It doesn't work. The only way to achieve a life that brings forth all that you seek is to live in two places: the *doing* and the *being*. Take time for stillness and time for action. Now let's better understand the value of both.

The Difference Between *Doing* and *Being*

Coaches and psychologists deliver the concept of *doing* versus *being* in many different ways. I have a thought process I use in my personal life, family life, and business. It has become a way of living and opened my mind to endless possibilities—including forgiveness.

To begin, it's important to know that neuroscience research has shown we actually have three brains: our head brain or "cephalic brain," our heart brain or "cardiac brain," and our gut brain or "enteric brain." Each of these brains is a complex information-processing center made of billions of neurons working in synchronicity.

- The *head brain* analyzes information and keeps us in a state of consciousness. It provides meaning and gives language to our life.
- The *heart brain* senses the world through emotions and feelings. Our values come from our heart as does our interpersonal relationships.
- The *gut brain* provides us with intuition and understanding of who we are in the world. From here we respond to danger, red flags, and life challenges.[1]

As a society, we've often been conditioned to make choices with our head, typically by analyzing numbers, behavior patterns, and data. But with forgiveness, it's important to feel your emotions and decide to forgive from your heart first, followed by your gut and mind. Let me explain why.

The heart has long been considered the source of love, feeling, bravery, and wisdom. The HeartMath Institute Research Center has been "exploring the physiological mechanisms by which the heart communicates with the brain, thereby influencing information processing, perceptions, emotions and health."[2] Their research has shown that our heart rhythms are "reflective of inner emotional states and stress." When we feel "low-vibe emotions," such as anger, resentment, and sadness, this causes an "increased disorder in the heart's rhythms and in the autonomic nervous system, thereby adversely affecting the rest of the body."[3] The opposite occurs when we feel "high-vibe emotions," such as joy, peace, and love: we experience a profound sense of harmony and calm within our bodies.

The HeartMath Institute observed that "the heart was acting as though it had a mind of its own and was profoundly influencing the way we perceive and respond to the world. In essence, it appeared that the heart was affecting intelligence and awareness" as well as "mental clarity, creativity, emotional balance, and personal effectiveness." We now realize the heart's "brain" is an information center that "processes emotions and communicates with our cranial brain via the nervous system, hormonal system, and other pathways."[4]

Thus, for the forgiveness process to work, our thoughts and words must connect with the emotions in our hearts. A grieving or hurt person who says, "I forgive you," from only their mind will never feel the deep release forgiveness affords. In contrast, someone who feels ready to let go of sadness and invite peace will experience the positive effects of forgiveness.

Let's delve deeper into these concepts. Have you ever been jealous of someone who has been able to forgive? Or perhaps you've noticed someone's joy and thought, *How did they let go of pain? I want what they have.* Maybe you've said, "I'd love to forgive, but I just can't." These doubts and questions appear when your belief and self-worth, which are needed to create change, aren't aligned with your actions. If you're struggling with self-worth and self-love, which come from the solar plexus and heart chakra, please go back and reread step three.

The process of forgiving cannot happen without believing peace and freedom override holding on to anger, sadness, and resentment for the person(s) who hurt you. When your head brain (meaning), heart brain (belief and self-love), and gut brain (understanding) align, you can trust and believe in your road to forgiveness. Choices are easier to make, fear dissipates, and faith takes precedence. This is why the balance of *being* and *doing* is so vital for forgiveness.

Many times when clients meet me for the first time on a video conference call, they're taken aback. They don't expect nature and heart-centered talk to be delivered from a mainstream single mom of three sons. But here's the thing: slowing your mind and connecting with your heart isn't touchy-feely nonsense.

One way I've been asking you to connect with your heart and body is through meditation. Since 2012, the number of people practicing meditation has tripled.[5] One reason is that during meditation, our frontal cortex, the part of the brain in charge of reasoning, planning, emotions, and self-awareness, often goes offline.[6] And in today's maxed-out world, many people are seeking ways to both mentally and physically slow down.

As you learned in the preface, the same happens to our brains when we spend time in nature: our prefrontal takes a rest, and our default network is allowed to rise. Florence Williams sources Ruth Ann Atchley, a psychologist from the University of Kansas, in her book *The Nature Fix*. Atchley stated, "My hypothesis is when you're engaged in nature, it leads to mindfulness. It's passive, the world is coming and going. It's so good for depression. When you walk out in nature, it's like wearing rose-colored glasses. In nature everything is a little more positive, there's a little more connectedness."[7] Therefore, it makes sense that *meditating in nature* has a profound impact on my clients.

Companies and top executives from the likes of Apple, Google, and Nike now encourage, offer, and practice daily meditation. For instance, Steve Jobs used Zen meditation to pursue enlightenment and simplicity.[8] Whether you agree with his style of creating and living, he's a prime example of an innovator and visionary who didn't believe in only *doing* to make life happen. He seemed to understand the necessity to become quiet within and listen to what's possible.

In a Stanford University commencement address, Jobs said, "Your time is limited, so don't waste it living someone else's life. Don't be trapped by dogma—which is living with the results of other people's thinking. Don't let the noise of others' opinions drown out your own inner voice. And most important, have the courage to follow your heart and intuition. They somehow already know what you truly want to become. Everything else is secondary."[9] In other words, Jobs encouraged the graduates to listen to their heightened intuition (gut brain) and the voice of their heart (heart brain).

In a society of overthinkers and taskmasters, we need to accept this idea of taking moments to slow our minds in our business, personal, and family lives. Sure, this state of being can feel unnatural at first. Meditating and being with myself was difficult after separating from my husband. My goal had been to never get divorced, so how could I change my fixation from *doing* anything to fix my marriage, to now *being* with the emotions that engulfed me? Especially when for *seventeen years* loyalty to my husband, our relationship, and our family had been stronger than devotion to myself. As hard as the reality was to accept, I knew the only way out of this stagnation was through it, and that meant being and sitting with every emotion. Embracing my feelings was tough. But once I began practicing meditation in nature, I could see and accept my feelings and responsibility for staying in a toxic relationship.

I'd like to share two important realizations that came to me while I was stand-up paddleboarding and meditating in the Pacific Ocean:

- One person cannot repair what it takes two people to work on, so quit trying.
- By constantly fixing others' mistakes, you're sabotaging their life lessons and responsibility for their actions, while dismissing your own life in the process.

Without having this clarity while meditating, I never would have fully released attachment from trying to mend my world.

These realizations provided insight to why I felt stuck in my relationship for so many years. *I was part of the problem.* I thought I could fix everything by being the best wife imaginable. I was a great partner and mother who kept the house clean, cared for the children, and did what I could to relieve my husband of extra stress. Understanding my role in our marriage fallout imparted knowledge I needed to honor my feelings and move into forgiveness for my husband and myself. It wasn't always comfortable being quiet with my thoughts. But I never would have reached this enlightened realization without slowing down my mind and dropping into my heart and body.

Unless you sit, become still, and embrace your fear, sadness, and/or rage, your actions won't result in the desired outcome. When stuck in this hamster-wheel conundrum of "I've tried this so many times and it never works" thought process, you become frustrated with life, resentful, and tempted to eventually give up.

As I mentioned, nature offers lessons we need in the moment and in life. We simply have to listen. In step two, I wrote about the way Eva connected with her inner warrior when hiking the trail became hard. Now I'd like to share her experience with *being* versus *doing* and the impact this had on her.

It was day five of our retreat. We were midway hiking out of the canyon when we came upon a creek with shade. Eva was struggling, and I could feel her concern. Eva was physically able to finish the hike, but her emotions weren't aligned with her mind, body, and spirit, making it extremely difficult to continue.

Imagine it like this: her mind was pushing her body forward, but her heart and emotions were a ball and chain being dragged along the trail. How grueling does that sound? Though fear and anxiety held her back, I knew that because she's a trauma survivor, she also carried anger, sadness, and loss. Once she settled into those emotions and released what she could, peace would manifest and she'd feel inspired to begin again. I had Eva lie in the creek, to let the water wash over her and cool her. Here's how she described the experience:

> As I got in the creek, my body instantly thanked me for the relief. We had been hiking in heat, and I was exhausted. As I relaxed into my body, Sara kept bringing me back to the present moment. She asked me to feel the water, take some deep breaths, clear all the thoughts, and just "be" in the moment. All I wanted was to "be." I was so physically exhausted from the "doing" in life. It was as if my body was pushed into the "being" because that is all that was left. I didn't want to move—ever—from this peaceful spot.

At times in our lives, we must secede from what's happening around us and be present with what we can control. I reminded Eva to breathe deeply from her belly, grounding herself to the rocks in the creek, while letting the water carry away her emotions. By doing so, some of her anger, frustration, and anxiety were released, while peace and acceptance settled in. Her self-love was fed in the process. We took important self-care time to relax, talk, feel into our bodies, and laugh before moving again and safely making it out of the canyon.

Carrying negative emotions is exhausting. I remember days when I felt like I was lugging around my fear, hatred, and resentment. I repeatedly tried to let go of these emotions, but I couldn't. It took me a while to trust that I wouldn't be carrying them forever. However, through the process of forgiving, I knew I eventually would be free of the toxicity I was holding. But I also realized forgiveness has its own timeline and I couldn't force anything to happen.

In the same way, Eva fought to climb up the mountain while also carrying many emotions. It was analogous to how she lived her daily life. She wanted to let go of her pain, but her body wasn't ready.

When carrying and processing through experiences and feelings, remember to self-soothe and be present, especially in a moment of exhaustion.

I'd like to share a process I use to balance *doing* and *being* in my life. Throughout this section, you'll find journal prompts that will help bring you back to alignment.

1. **NOTICE YOUR EMOTIONS AND WHERE THEY LAND IN YOUR BODY.**

   Pay attention when you're feeling triggered by something. What emotions come up for you? And where are they landing in your body? Does this trigger push you into control, fight, flight, or freeze mode? Or does this trigger bring up sadness, depression, or a need to retreat or avoid? Whatever the case, journal where the emotion is present.

   All of this information becomes data for your life. As discussed earlier in this chapter, your head, heart, and gut brains function and share information with one another. You need to listen and notice what's coming up within your body before you can do something about it. It's also beneficial to observe and journal the patterns that cause triggers so you can understand how best to create boundaries in order to stop unhealthy behaviors. For example, if someone triggers you via text multiple times, it's your responsibility to create a boundary that prevents unnecessary exposure to that trigger. If you need a refresher about boundaries, revisit step four.

2. **GROUND YOURSELF AND HUG YOUR HEAD, HEART, OR GUT.**

   I love this part of the process. Once you determine where an emotion is settling in your body, stop what you're doing and take a pause. Place your hands over your head, heart, or gut, wherever the emotion is felt.

   I notice that when I'm triggered, most anger, resentment, and questioning lands in my head. Emotions of sadness, pain, grief, and heartache are in my heart. And hopelessness, fear, abandonment, shame, and regret usually process through my gut.

   Once your hands are situated, close your eyes, direct your attention, and be present. Take a deep breath. Now imagine a miniature version of you wrapping its arms around your head, heart, or gut, giving it a long hug. Can this little version of you hug even a bit harder and longer? Most clients will cry, laugh, or even scream during this experience. All I ask is that you give yourself permission to feel emotional release. Whatever comes out is meant to happen. This is simple yet powerful.

3. **ASK YOURSELF, *WHAT ARE MY NEEDS RIGHT NOW? AND WHAT CAN I DO OR HOW CAN I BE IN ORDER TO GET MY NEEDS MET?***

It's crucial to understand your needs. And yes, your needs are as important as anyone else's. Acknowledging your commitment to self in this way will deepen your love and worthiness, both requirements on your road to forgiveness.

Please ask these questions while visualizing your mini-self hugging your head, heart, or gut. Journal your responses:

—What are my needs right now?

—What can I do to get my needs met?

If you're someone who is constantly in motion, can you find five minutes of "soft fascination" a day to sit in silence, go for a walk, or lie down and read a book? And if you're someone who is having trouble stepping into action, can you set intentions, create small benchmarks, or go back to your values and ask, "What am I dishonoring by holding myself back?"

Get excited for what happens when you step into fierce self-compassion and self-love. Let's agree to slow down, be still with emotions, honor your needs, and allow life to happen without feeling the need to control every moment out of anxiety or fear. Are you ready for this new way of living? I believe you are.

Let Go of the Heavy, Unwanted Things You Are Carrying in Life

Every time I stand on the rim of the Grand Canyon, I look over it in complete awe. Yes, I'm overcome by the beauty. But many times it's the expansiveness that truly affects me. There's a spiritual energy in this vast, empty space that I haven't found anywhere else in the world.

I remember my first time walking to the edge. There was a dichotomy of feeling so small, yet larger than life. Observing the birds soar high over the cliffs and dwellings fostered my own sense of freedom in my body. What if we could feel that much peace and glide with the winds every day? How would it feel not to be weighed down in life? To only carry what's needed for our daily existence?

These obscure thoughts entered my mind years before I discovered my husband was betraying me. No doubt, the demons he carried throughout our time together were heavy. And though I didn't realize it at the time, the toxic energy I carried because of his behavior also weighed me down. As hard as it was to hear my husband's truth, it released me from the shackles of his secrets. I imagine that you, or someone you know, has carried secrets, betrayals, or lies you were unaware of. Or perhaps you chose to carry them out of guilt, shame, responsibility, or fear. Many of us learn to compartmentalize our emotions, or we ignore the damage that carrying excess baggage will do to us. Regardless of the past, I'm grateful the father of my kids didn't overdose and that I didn't contract a disease while he risked our lives through his actions.

Forgiveness is a beautiful practice for many reasons. But one of the greatest benefits is the opportunity to choose what you carry in life. It's easy to say yes to what fulfills your days. But remember, even when difficult times arise in your life, you get to decide when you let go of those too.

Here is a perfect analogy. In 2014, I was hiking a trail in Sequoia National Park with friends when one of the guys thought it would be funny to sneak big rocks into my pack. The first time it happened I returned from the bushes and threw my pack over my shoulder, not noticing the extra weight. When we stopped for lunch, I reached in to grab my sandwich and pulled out multiple large rocks. I laughed and found it kind of funny. And then it happened a second time. Yes, this was a prank being played on me, but it wasn't until the third or fourth time that I realized the rock-filled pack was a metaphor of my life.

When you make yourself vulnerable—without safe boundaries excluding what or who cannot be trusted—inevitably you will walk away carrying something you didn't choose. Many times we don't realize the people closest to us can't be trusted. But when you're aware, decisions can be made. It's your right and responsibility to create a life you love and in the process make it lighter.

We'll continue with the hiking pack analogy to decide what we don't feel like carrying any longer. I like to use this with all of my clients, both hikers and nonhikers.

As I say to my clients when preparing for our hike, "You determine what you need to carry in your pack." I make sure everyone has necessities, but how they fill the remainder of the pack is their responsibility. I've had clients carry large Vidal Sassoon hair dryers, beautiful lingerie, and expensive makeup. No judgment from me! I've carried floaties for the river, Dom Pérignon, Christmas lights, birthday decorations, and of course, my red high heels for photo opportunities in nature. The list is crazy, but I love having fun. That said, I also refuse to carry out what others choose to take in.

I use our hiking packs as a metaphor for the material things we hold on to in life. I'm a firm believer in owning items that touch our hearts and souls. Why carry and care for things that don't matter or serve us?

I mentioned earlier that my boys and I sold our house and most of our belongings in 2017. I wanted to create a new home filled with intention and connection. To do that, we had to reevaluate where we lived and note what we kept around us. We need items for safety, survival, and happiness. But what if we could let go of the things that dragged us down every day? How would it feel to unload baggage from an ex-lover or a failed relationship?

Some people—including me—believe that items in our possession hold energy, memories, and attachment to us. Like when you wear your grandmother's ring and feel her presence. Or when you sit in your father's favorite chair and can sense he is with you. Feeling energy in objects is called *psychometry*. Psychometry is the "practice of reading, or sensing, the history of an object and its owner through touch."[10] To fully detach from another human, experience, or time in your life, you must be ready to let go of the items holding connection. I sold what was once my dream home for that reason. No amount of *feng shui* (a Chinese method of arranging a room to harmonize the space with its occupant) or "smudging" (a traditional Native American method of burning sacred herbs to cleanse or purify a space) could rid my house of the energy that connected my present life to my past. I had to physically detach, and it was hard. Even so, I knew that by letting go, I was inviting new possibilities and memories to be created on my terms, not within four walls I'd purchased with my ex-husband.

DO LESS + BE MORE

I'd like you to do an exercise, some of which I did with my boys when we moved. Please journal what comes up for you. Let's start with a meditation I'd like you to do inside your house, where most of your belongings are. Be in a place in your home that has both meaning and connection. Where do you spend most of your time? Perhaps it's your bedroom or kitchen. In this space, sit either on the floor or in a chair.

Guided Meditation for Letting Go of Possessions

Close your eyes.

Place your hands over your heart and take a deep breath in.

Release your breath.

Notice the energy of the space surrounding you.

Is there a vibe of happiness and joy? Or do you feel sadness and anger?

Continue taking slow, deep breaths.

Does being here make you want to escape or be present?

Do you want to leave this space? Do you love this space?

Now open your eyes if they are closed and sit in the stillness.

Take notice of what material items are around you.

Look at the shelves and notice what you see.

One by one, observe each item while asking yourself these questions:

Does this item touch my heart and soul?

Why does this item mean so much to me?

Do I need this item to feel safe or live my daily life?

Would I feel lighter if I let go of this unwanted, unused, or unneeded item?

If something has meaning, expect to answer these questions quickly. If you take longer to answer, there's probably a reason, and perhaps it's time to let that thing go.

> Now pick up your journal and start a list of objects you're ready to give away.

Complete this exercise with every room in your house. Please go at your own pace. For instance, I did this exercise over the course of a month. At some point you may be ready to ask, "Is this my home? Or am I ready to let go of this house and move into a new home?" I view four walls as just a house. But a home is something you create, with positive energy, laughter, and material items that have meaning. Thus, if you experienced trauma such as betrayal or abuse, or if you had an unhappy marriage in this space, perhaps it's time to detach from your house and create the home you've always dreamed about.

It's okay if this idea overwhelms you. If this pursuit is something you'd like to explore but are afraid, I suggest going back to step five and using the comfort zone practice. You may be surprised how ready you are.

Now that you've detached from physical items that don't make you happy or hold meaning, I'd like to discuss releasing emotional and mental baggage. Doesn't that sound freeing? Begin by imagining that you carry a "life pack," a backpack that holds experiences you've lived through, memories, tools for life, and learnings from your past. Your life pack also holds everything from your present, future goals, ambitions, relationships with your family and friends, hurt and pain, as well as happiness and joy. There are responsibilities for jobs, careers, your kids, and pets. Not to mention obligations for home, philanthropy, and volunteer work. Whoa—suddenly this pack sounds, looks, and feels kind of big, doesn't it?

The question is: What are you carrying that doesn't belong to you? Many times we find ourselves holding on to consequences from others' actions; emotions that don't serve us; or worries, anxiety, and fear that prohibit us from living our best lives. We may be guilt-ridden or shamed into doing what isn't in our best interests or doesn't align with our values. My hope is for you to decipher what you need, and what you're ready and willing to let go of, in order to move into forgiveness. You deserve to lighten your load. And by unpacking what isn't bringing happiness, you make room for new memories and experiences, joy and peace.

As I continue to guide you through these steps, understand that there's no judgment. If you cannot let go of the resentment, pain, or anything else in life right now, that's okay. Stay open to the possibility and continue using the tools I've given you. As mentioned before, please don't force your forgiveness journey. Be good to yourself and practice self-care. Take walks and journal. When you need a hug, wrap your arms around yourself and be fiercely self-compassionate. You'll know when you're ready to let go of physical items and emotional pain—you simply have to listen to your inner voice. We've talked about this throughout the book. When you hear or receive a message in your mind, heart, or "gut brain" that you're ready to let go, stop for a moment, take a breath, and ask yourself, *Am I ready to let go?*

Let's do an exercise that will help determine what to carry in your life pack. We'll begin with a guided visualization, followed by journal prompts. If possible, I'd like you to go outdoors and begin by grounding yourself in nature. Lean against a tree, lie on the grass, or put your feet in the sand.

Guided Visualization for Your Life Pack

Take a deep breath.

And release.

Let the earth hold your body.

You are safe.

Take another deep breath in.

And release.

Now imagine you are standing on a hill surrounded by rolling fields and plains.

You look at the landscape in awe.

A sense of freedom comes over you. There is so much beauty. Tall grass dances in the breeze. Butterflies and birds float with the wind. Everything feels serene.

Your eyes meet a creek with slow-moving water, and you trace its path through the valley. You notice each turn it takes as it snakes its way through the earth.

Where does this creek go? Where does its path lead?

Your curiosity makes you wonder what else is out there. You want to experience what's beyond the view you currently see.

You can see the path—but where else does it go?

If you simply follow the trail carved out by nature, you will be guided to the endless possibilities the world has to offer. It's just a matter of taking the steps.

And the thought enters your mind: *If I have a way to get there, what is holding me back?*

You feel a little excitement.

Why not experience all the possibilities the world has to offer?

Looking down at this path, you decide to head that way next. There's no reason not to. Your mind begins opening to new ideas. To all the possibilities that are out there for you. You wonder, *If I can say yes to taking one step at a time, what else can I say yes to? Is it possible to experience life a little lighter? A little freer?*

Take another breath in.

Place your hands over your heart.

And release your breath.

Continue to ask yourself, *Can I let go of the emotional and mental baggage that does not belong to me? Can I release the consequences of others' actions that I have been carrying? Am I holding myself responsible for another person's behavior?*

You realize something important: you have choice.

There are roads and paths and trails to take you anywhere in life. It is your responsibility to take the first step and to decide what you choose to carry.

Breathe in.

Feel your heartbeat.

Release your breath. And gently open your eyes.

Think back to your values and inner warrior from step two.

Bring them both to the present moment and tap into that inner knowing whenever you need it.

Take some time to journal the answers to these questions. Use your values and inner warrior from step two to guide you in this process. Remember, both are there to help you make healthy decisions for a life you choose.

- What is necessary for a fulfilled life?
- What are my desires?
- What is possible for my future, by holding only what is mine?
- How will it feel to relieve myself of the responsibility to fix what I cannot control?
- How will those closest to me benefit by me putting myself first?
- Complete this sentence: I am ready to let go of _____.

These questions may not be easy to answer, and completing the above sentence may be especially hard right now. Take some time to journal your answers from your heart chakra and solar plexus, and not only your head. As a reminder, your heart and solar plexus are the source of your love, values, and intuition. Your answers should align with all of these.

I invite you to use this visualization as a weekly practice. You may find some days that you're unwilling to let go of a strong emotion or thought. And other days you are. The point is that your life pack is forever being unpacked and repacked! The beautiful part is there's no right or wrong way to do so. I encourage you to think about carrying more happiness than sadness, more joy than anger, and more peace than resentment. When experiencing high-vibe emotions, we tend to invite more in because they feel good, which is a light way to live. And this is ultimately what I hope for you!

Stop Fighting and Stop Overcomplicating Life

I was recently the guest on a podcast talking about forgiveness. The host asked, "What tool would you like to leave with our listeners?" I thought of you, me, all of us—the whole world. We are in a critical time. There's so much unrest and many contentious issues abound: politics, border control, climate change, and pandemics.

My reply to the host was, "Keep life simple and lead with kindness."

In this moment, if we choose to do so, we have an opportunity to unite for a greater good. During crises, we decide how to show up in the world. My hope is that through experiencing contention in society, we learn the value of all human life, we think about how our actions affect others, and we lead with a calm mind while learning from others' examples. Through acts of love and kindness for one another, ourselves, and this world, we heal. And this mentality applies to everything in life.

Whether we're dealing with traumas, feeling lost or isolated, or unsure of our next steps, remember that clarity won't come when we're in turmoil. Fighting and drama create a more complicated life, whereas slowing down in a time of crisis and being still in the moment bring simplicity to life. Go outside and take a walk. Breathe and ground yourself. Pass someone on the street and smile. See what happens when you do.

I often ask myself this question: *How can I make my life more simple?* And nearly every time I hear, *Let go.*

You have come so far and I am proud of you! In step seven, our final step, I'll discuss forgiveness. Together, we can change the world with this beautiful practice.

STEP SEVEN

Practice Forgiveness

Forgiveness will save your life. It saved mine.

I don't credit the police, church, or the government for protecting me. Neither my social worker, coach, nor support group taught me the tool that transformed my existence. My family and friends were helpful and supportive, but they couldn't guide me to this place of healing and recovery. I had to learn how to let go of my deepest pain and forgive on my own.

I never set out to be a thought leader on forgiveness. It would be far easier to ghost the world and live an introverted, private, contented life, but that wasn't meant to be. I've learned that my voice, ideas, and stories matter. People deserve to heal and move on. Our traumas have affected families, colleagues, friends, communities, and most importantly, our children. My unconventional healing journey has worked for me, and I know it can work for you.

Finding my voice through this process has been like walking

through mud. I've looked up to thought leaders such as Glennon Doyle, Elizabeth Gilbert, Gabby Bernstein, Brené Brown, and Cheryl Strayed, all storytellers with wise words. Their books discuss addiction, pain, nature, motherhood, finding yourself, uncovering truth, sexuality, and intimacy, all topics I relate to. I've laughed and cried while highlighting paragraphs and journaling entries. What better way to gain insight into your life than by reading about and learning from others? In days of feeling sluggish and uneasy, I take a dose of courage and keep trekking along.

I'd like to write the last step of this book in honor of you for showing up and committing to this journey. You've done a brilliant job with steps one through six. Remember that this book isn't meant to be put on a shelf and forgotten about. I'd love to see you use it over and over, to continue deepening your relationship with yourself. Highlight what works and cross out what doesn't. Take notes in the margins, and perhaps leave annotations for your kids or grandkids to learn from, whether now or in the future. If you struggled with any of the steps, give yourself some time and revisit these at a later date. I do the work every day.

Here is a recap of where we've traveled together thus far:

Step 1: Set your intention and surrender. Have fun in life, including on this forgiveness journey. We all have an inner child wanting to play and learn. Invite that child in. Release low-vibe emotions, such as sadness, anger, and fear, and replace them with high-vibe emotions, such as happiness, joy, and freedom. Take the pressure off yourself when making choices in life. Be good to you. Set your intentions for this work, but don't attach to the outcome. Surrender and enjoy the process.

Step 2: Ask, "Who am I?" You now have two important life tools: your values and your inner warrior. Your values help you make healthy, productive choices. And your inner warrior is the internal power, energy, and strength used to guide you. Understanding the core of who you are will make stepping into forgiveness far easier and more meaningful.

Step 3: Embrace self-worth + self-love. Traumatic experiences will greatly affect your self-worth and self-love. That's why it's important to establish a relationship with yourself. Love and honor your heart, mind, spirit, and soul. Get to know your inner critic. When it speaks, pause to hear if its words are valid or false. By choosing forgiveness every day, you deepen your self-worth and self-love.

Step 4: Set boundaries for yourself. Coming out of difficult experiences can lead to feeling unsafe and uncertain. Relationships may be fluid while establishing a new way of living. The only way to step into forgiveness and create a life you love is by setting proactive, healthy boundaries for yourself.

Step 5: Persevere when the work becomes hard. It's important to notice what you're comfortable with in life, and what you aren't. Learning to reframe stories and judgments in your head gives you strength to get through hard times. Forgiveness isn't always comfortable. Understanding what to do when it gets uncomfortable is key.

Step 6: Do less + be more. Balancing your *doing* state with your *being* state is powerful for healing. Slowing down brings clarity during chaotic times. Likewise, to set life into motion from a positive place, you must understand your needs. Forgiving others lets you release responsibility for their actions, recovery, pain, and responsibilities.

lh

Loving and taking care of people you care about requires you to first love and take care of yourself. That's why I refuse to hold guilt or shame for tending to my needs. As a survivor of PTSD and trauma, I know my boys need a whole mom, not pieces of a mom.

However, the work is ongoing. Every step within this book has led you to become a new version of yourself. A wiser, deeply emerging, loving human being who looks at yourself, the world, and life in a different way. That is my hope.

Practicing forgiveness is required to heal. You cannot fully experience a new way of living without letting go of what doesn't serve you well today. It's a road less traveled, this "unbecoming to become," and one I pray will become more utilized in this world.

So how do you begin? It starts with looking in the mirror. In this step, you will:

- Learn how to forgive yourself. For so long, I beat myself up with a ruminating question: How could I have gotten to this place in my life? I grappled with shame and regret for not listening to my heart and intuition. And it hurts to live with the consequences of one's mistakes. I had to work through many layers of pain to understand what happened. Once I started down the path of unbecoming a partner to becoming a new me, I was able to forgive myself, let go of the "how," and practice self-compassion. I'll forever be on this self-forgiveness journey, and I look forward to teaching you what I've learned along the way.
- Learn how to forgive others. After I forgave myself, I sought to forgive others, which requires diligence and courage. By handing back the pain to those who have betrayed, assaulted, and abused me, I regained my strength, power, and belief in

self. I found my voice and, with that, a new piece of myself that I love and admire. I was born to teach you this process!

- Learn how to forgive the world. Society has difficulty grasping a situation like mine. And other people have difficulty understanding anything they've never personally experienced. I've handed back the humiliation and judgment foisted on me as a teenage sexual assault victim, an unwed teen mother, and a betrayed and abused partner by going public with my story, speaking on the TEDx Manhattan Beach stage, and writing a book. I've chosen to forgive and to educate the world so others don't feel condemned as I once did. We're all called to do and be better.

- Listen to a meditation that will guide you through a three-part forgiveness journey for self, others, and the world. Brittany Lynne is a mindfulness and meditation teacher who assists on my Grand Canyon retreats. Together, we created this beautiful meditation for all of you. This meditation brings me to tears every time I listen to it. I'm grateful to have an opportunity to bring it to you.

Since I started writing this book, our world has experienced multiple upheavals. We are being forced to do less and be more—to listen and to learn—exactly what I wrote about in step six. Some days I wonder if this book isn't writing itself in a strange sort of way, like it's playing out in front of me, chapter by chapter.

For instance, I was outside with my dog during our government stay-at-home order when a neighbor stopped by. Standing six feet away—the recommended protocol for social distancing—he said, "Sara, I took my board to the beach today and stood at the water's edge. For the first time in years, I didn't feel the pressures of life. I watched ripples in the ocean and looked at the sand. I saw things I hadn't noticed before." He paused and shook his head. "It was like . . . different! It was peaceful." His eyes were wide, and his speech was slow.

I smiled, recognizing his childlike sense at his experience. This was the first thing I talked about in step one. Sitting in awe, playing, exploring, and having fun is healing. Our brains are given space to rest, and our anxieties decrease. We begin noticing details that were there all along, such as ripples in the ocean and tiny grains of sand. I responded to my neighbor, "Yes, that's what I did for the first three years of my recovery. You didn't only look at nature. You observed and felt it. You connected with something deeper than yourself."

In a life of being busy and task-mastering, we're being handed a season to slow down. Those who surrender and accept it as a gift will find lessons. Those who fight what's happening will feel anxiety, frustration, and fear of what's out of our control.

In my family, my twelfth- and eighth-grade sons' last few months of school have been eradicated. Neither of them will walk the halls with friends for the last day of school. My high school senior won't experience his final sports competition or be handed his diploma at graduation. It's sad. Yet, perhaps because they're accustomed to learning from traumas, my boys are finding peace within the storm that's swirling around us. We cannot control pandemics, natural disasters, or how others live their lives. But we do have an opportunity to uplevel outside of the chaos. And this is where forgiveness fits in.

How to Forgive Yourself

Finding out I was pregnant after being raped was the single most scary moment of my young adult life. No one had to criticize, judge, or scold me for what happened. I was hard enough on myself for "being at the wrong place at the wrong time," even though I knew it wasn't my fault. In a way, I felt like I'd let myself down. In fact, a part of me believed I'd let my entire family down. I wondered how my grandparents would take the news and if they would blame my parents for not "protecting" me. I wondered how my Catholic extended family would view me, how my teachers would react, and for God's sake, who would ever want to date a girl who was raped and had a child?

My early days of pregnancy were filled with regret, sadness, rage, anxiety, and fear. The possibility to compete at state in track and field was gone. Any plans I had to apply to colleges outside of the area also disappeared. I found myself drowning in a sea of disappointment. And to make matters worse, I felt I was part of the cause.

Through the months, as my belly grew, slivers of hope thankfully appeared like a rainbow after a storm. Taking walks in the countryside or working on my art, I found peace while dreaming of possibilities. Ever so slowly I began to like myself again. I accepted my new reality and began to secretly plan my future. I'd think, *If I live out my life with just me and my baby, that's okay. We don't need much.* Sometimes I'd share thoughts with my parents, and other times I kept my thoughts to myself.

At some point I decided to continue with college and become an art teacher, blending my passions of teaching, art, and kids. I didn't have all of the answers, but I knew my direction. Life kept moving forward because that's what I needed. Then one day I had a spiritual awakening while lying on the bathroom floor after a good sob session. I heard the words, *The only way to heal and love you and your unborn baby is to forgive yourself for what happened.* Of course I knew I hadn't done anything wrong or caused what happened. But it was time to release guilt for being at the wrong place at the wrong time. I had to let go of the shame I felt for knowing the person who did this to me. And I needed to stop feeling like I could have done more to stop it. The question of, "Why didn't I . . . ?" had to end. Ultimately, I needed to quit blaming myself for my perpetrator's actions and for society's unwillingness to believe me.

It's not uncommon for victims to hold blame when bad things happen. I see it all of the time with clients who feel responsible for something that happened, sometimes years prior, when they aren't to blame. Michelle Pinedo was one of those clients.

✍

Michelle chose to share her story during the filming of the documentary *Walk Through This: A Story of Starting Over* in the Grand Canyon. This beautiful thirty-seven-year-old woman lost her fiancé, Kelvin, in a tragic car accident in December 2014, when he fell asleep at the wheel. His parents, his sister, and Michelle didn't find out until the next morning. She then lost her younger sister, Angelina, in a hit-and-run car accident in January 2019. While coming home from a party one night, Angelina was walking right behind Michelle as they crossed the street. In a split second, she was stuck by a driver that fled. Michelle tried to save her with CPR, but Angelina died at the scene. PTSD from Angelina's death brought up emotions and memories from Kelvin's death.

Michelle joined us for the filming, as she says, "without expectations, but hoping to find physical anger and release it for what happened to Angelina," especially after court hearings that didn't prove in her family's favor. Hiking down the South Kaibab trail, we were deep in conversation about the accident when I asked her, "Michelle, do you think what happened to Angelina was your fault?" She stopped, and I wondered if I'd pushed it too far with my question.

"I was not expecting that." She looked angry and confused. "Sh*t, Sara!"

I smiled softly and shook my head. That was *exactly* what she needed to be asked. "Hon, it wasn't your fault," I told her. "It's okay to forgive."

"But I came here to find anger. I thought I would throw rocks over the edge or scream into the canyon. This isn't what I came here to do! I didn't come here to process forgiveness."

Nature will always give us what we need. Sometimes it's what we least expect. Being on the trail provided space and time for Michelle to find clarity within this tragic situation.

I recently spoke with Michelle about her experience. She shared the following with me:

I had so much guilt that was involved with Angelina passing. I needed to start to forgive myself. It was such a huge step because we are our hardest critic. I was beating myself up over it every single day to the point that I didn't think I'd still be alive. . . .

Since the canyon, I've been putting in the work. And

it's very different from how I processed the first death. With Kelvin, I was angry and didn't process or do the work. I was drinking and doing things to avoid the processing. I felt like a shi**y person. With Angelina, I am doing the work so I don't go down the same path as before. I am trying to heal myself in a better way. There are a lot of moments that I am discovering and feeling peace. I allow myself to feel the low moments, but I don't allow myself to stay there.[1]

Let's get real. We all make mistakes, yet society can be quick to accuse victims. "Why did you have that extra drink?" "What were you wearing?" "Why didn't you go to the doctor sooner?" "Why were you at the party?" We even question the abused: "Why did you keep going back to the man who hurt you?" Every time victims hear an accusatory question, they step back into shame, guilt, and regret. The further we step back from anything in life, the harder it is to step forward.

The judgment must stop.

Victims carry their stories and stigma in life, unsure why there's a constant fog or cloud looming. They find themselves in one toxic job or relationship after another, not understanding why they "can't get happiness right." Here is what I know: patterns of behavior and unhealthy relationships will never change until you address your pain, let go of your past, and forgive yourself.

Many clients confess, "It's so hard to do. And scary."

It's easy to understand why, especially when we assume responsibility for an experience we didn't ask for. That, right there, is why we start with forgiveness for self: to accept responsibility where we can, learn from our experiences, release pain, and regain our power. We forgive ourselves for one of two reasons:

1. We wronged another person or did something we know isn't right, and we're ready to acknowledge and learn from our mistakes.

2. We've been holding on to shame, guilt, and remorse for something that happened to us, yet the fault isn't ours to hold. Instead, let's assume responsibility for what *is* ours, learn what we can from the situation, and let go of the pain.

Self-forgiveness is a beautiful tool. Please do not think of it as a task, because it isn't. It's a gift to look at yourself in the mirror with love and compassion, to witness your beautiful soul and say, "I forgive you." Getting there takes time and patience. Much of what I am about to share must be practiced daily, especially if you have experienced a tremendous amount of PTSD.

I begin my day in forgiveness with the following five-part process that includes journal prompts. If I'm on my board on the Pacific Ocean or on a trail and cannot journal my thoughts, I use my phone to record or transcribe my words. Find your place in the world where you like to work on forgiveness, and make this space your own.

Part One: Acknowledge Your Mistakes and Recognize the Pain They Caused

Our mistakes are turned into lessons through our learning process. Every situation or experience in our lives provides opportunity for growth. I cringe when people say to me, "One hundred percent responsibility is placed on David for your divorce." Yes, my husband betrayed me and caused the demise of our relationship. However, I made plenty of mistakes in my marriage, including fostering codependency in our relationship and inflicting pain on myself for refusing to let go. When my mom tried to tell me something felt amiss in my marriage, I automatically shut down and dismissed her. I desperately wanted the marriage I had dreamed about as a little girl. The one I thought had flown out the window when I was raped at seventeen. When I met David, he automatically became my best friend and breathed life into a part of my world I thought was gone. What I didn't realize at the time was that he showed me what was possible. But it wasn't possible with him.

Remember throughout this process of self-forgiveness that we're all human beings doing the best we can, using the tools we know. No one is perfect.

Let's start by taking ownership of your mistakes and the pain they have caused. Perhaps you've hurt another person, lied to your boss, cheated on an exam, or gotten mad at someone without reason. You may need to confront stigmas from your past that you've been holding on to. You can seek forgiveness for anything at any time. Go back in your life as far as you need to go. If it's something you have been carrying, now may be the time to look at it. You just need to be ready.

In your journal, complete this sentence for every mistake you're reflecting on:
I am responsible for _____.
My mistakes caused pain to _____ because _____.

I completed these sentences like this:

I am responsible for not heeding signs of my husband's infidelity while we were married. From the nights he showed up late from work, text messages from numbers I didn't recognize, his irrational behaviors, to the (many) times I questioned our lack of intimacy.

My mistakes caused pain to me and our children. *Because* I chose to set aside reappearing red flags, I stayed in a marriage that wasn't authentic or balanced. I lost time in my life for a meaningful, loving, intimate relationship. Consequently, our children haven't witnessed the love between parents that I'd hoped for.

Part Two: Take Note of What Caused the Incident

We need to "unpack" events and understand what caused our divorces, losses, deaths, misunderstandings, frayed friendships, and other problems. It's crucial to ask yourself, *Why did it occur?* and *What could I have done differently?* It's also important to take note of details—with both victims and perpetrators—surrounding difficult events. Again, ask yourself, *Was I in a stressful time of my life? Were there kids involved?*

Life should be created by new pathways toward your future, not in footsteps from your past. But you must be honest when answering these questions. By looking at the core of what happened and why it occurred, you deepen your relationship with self and connect in a more vulnerable, authentic way with others.

> Complete these sentences in your journal, using the mistake(s) you wrote about:
> The mistake or incident was caused by _____.
> It occurred because _____.
> I would have done this differently by _____.

I completed these sentences as follows:

The demise of our marriage was caused by my husband's betrayals and my diminished self-worth. He was dishonest with himself, me, and his children when he denied his true sexuality. On my part, I chose to listen to my husband instead of myself when I felt he was distant in our marriage. When I questioned his feelings and whereabouts, I placed his worthiness above my own.

This occurred because of my own issues with intimacy, caused by the trauma of rape at seventeen. Looking back, I see it clear as day. Had I taken an honest look at my younger self and given her pain the attention it deserved, I most likely would not have felt the need to find love and attention from someone else. My worthiness would have been enough, and I could have stood alone and still felt loved.

I would have approached my relationship with David differently by first working on myself before making a commitment to us both. It takes two fully healed individuals to create a healthy marriage. Both David and I were broken. We needed to learn to love ourselves for very different reasons. Had I approached our relationship like that, I believe our love for each other would have remained what it was intended for: love as friends, not as lovers.

Part Three: What Lessons Did You Learn? What Will You Do Differently in the Future?

Research shows that people who practice forgiveness tend to have healthier relationships.[2] Remember, that includes the relationship within yourself. By learning from your mistakes and letting go of low-vibe emotions, you can create a happier life by changing your behaviors. Through this process, you may notice a shift in how you approach friendships and family members. This is good! Writing down what you learned, or stating it out loud, can generate feelings of pain, exhilaration, or both. You are owning your power by receiving lessons and stating how you will follow them into a new future.

> Complete these sentences in your journal, again using the mistakes you wrote about:
> What I learned from my mistake was _____.
> What I will do differently in my life is _____.

I filled out these sentences like this:

My mistakes in our marriage taught me that I'm deserving of healthy, loving, intimate, and beautiful relationships. My life only has space for drama-free, authentic connections with friends, family members, colleagues, and people in my inner circle. I'm worthy of self-love, honesty, truth, compassion, and a partner in my life who carries the same values as my own. By working on myself to create the life and love I seek, I am showing my boys that no one is perfect and mistakes are lessons to be learned from. Having healthy boundaries is key.

I live my life very differently than my past and will continue to do so. When red flags appear, I take a moment to listen, process, and discern what is happening. Every day I have a choice to live without regret and with peace. I do not chase anyone or anything. Instead, I believe that life is unfolding for me, not to me. I wake in gratitude and live with intention.

Part Four: Forgive Yourself

You have taken ownership of your mistakes, stated what you learned, and established what you will do differently. Great job! Now it's time to release the shame, guilt, and pain associated with the events.

Think back to your intention from step one. Why did you open this book and choose this path? You've been doing a lot of inner work on this journey. Connect with your values and your inner warrior. Ask yourself, *What parts of me am I honoring by stepping into my higher self with forgiveness?* You will not only welcome freedom and peace but deepen your self-worth, love, relationships, and purpose in life.

> Complete this sentence in your journal and recite it every day. You can do this either in the mirror while making eye contact with yourself or in silence while sitting with your hands over your heart:
>
> I forgive myself for _____.
>
> I accept what I have learned from this situation. I release the shame, guilt, and pain I have held on to. I welcome happiness, peace, freedom, and calm. And I will do better by me, those around me, and the world. I forgive myself.

Let the words sink into your heart and soul while you feel the forgiveness wash over you. Imagine your shame, guilt, and pain leaving your body.

Part Five: Apologize and Attempt to Make Amends

This piece is to be used if you wronged someone else. If this is you, I commend and thank you for trying to seek forgiveness and apologize. Many times people who wrong others prefer to ignore the pain they inflicted, deflect what happened, or choose not to take responsibility for their actions. Yes, sometimes that's an easier way out, but that doesn't make it right. It's always better to take care of the issue at hand than to push it aside. Problems only grow when they aren't addressed.

Let me start by saying that the person you hurt may or may not accept your apology in the moment. Either way is fine. We're all on our own journeys in life, and you cannot force someone to accept anything. You may need to give them time to process your offering. This is a part of their own work in life. And, depending on your relationship with the person you hurt, be prepared to offer your apology several times, *without force*, while proving through actions that you are sorry.

Depending on your apology, your offer will come across one of two ways. So please make sure you are ready to apologize, with empathy, before you do so.

- If your apology is sincere, intentional for the person you wronged, and wrapped in love, you are creating space for a positive response.
- If your apology is forced, with a self-serving purpose, and intended for selfish reasons instead of selfless reasons, you are further insulting your victim. It will be far more difficult to come to a future resolution.

As victims, we hope that those who wronged us will feel remorse and say, "I'm sorry." In Michelle's case, that never happened. Angelina and her offender were the same age, so Michelle went into hearings and the court case with this mindset: "[The hit-and-run driver] was younger and perhaps didn't have the same beautiful childhood, family values, upbringing, love, supportive environment, or compassion that we grew up with." In spite of Michelle's willingness to be gracious toward the offender, the situation didn't go as she envisioned: "When she was so unremorseful, it baffled me and made everything very frustrating. I didn't know how to process or take that."

Michelle is continuing to work through this piece, and she said, "I would never wish her harm. I truly hope at some point she will have a lifestyle change and do some good."[3]

As offenders, it's equally important to do the work and take responsibility for your actions. You help yourself while also allowing others to grieve and find forgiveness. And in the process, offenders can be of service to the world.

I encourage my clients to write an apology letter to the person they wronged. You could also use this exercise as part of your own self-forgiveness process and write a letter to yourself. You may choose to mail the letter (I've mailed letters to myself from public mailboxes), or sit down with the person you hurt and read it to him or her (you also can read the letter aloud to yourself). Emailing is fine, but a handwritten letter is preferable. Seeing the personal words you created, in your unique handwriting, is far more powerful and meaningful than words transcribed through a keyboard. Your letter should include the following:

- Start with an apology. Use an intentional "I am" statement: I am sorry for _____.
- Own your mistake and what you did wrong. Be honest, forthcoming, and vulnerable. Explain what you would do differently now compared to then.

- Be empathetic with your words. Put yourself in the other person's shoes. Imagine what it must have been like for them to be wronged.
- Explain what you learned and what you are doing differently as you move forward.
- Admit "I was wrong," and ask for forgiveness.

Self-forgiveness is a commitment and requires daily work, but the rewards far exceed being stuck in self-punishment. By understanding, learning, and changing our courses in life, we create better and stronger friendships, families, and communities. I'm not condoning or excusing when we hurt others, or when others create pain for us. But we all make mistakes. It's what we do with what happened that matters.

How to Forgive Others

In the introduction, I shared how it felt to hear my husband disclose his betrayals and deceits. To have your world destroyed by the person you love is devastating. I was so angry, but what I said in response to his confessions shocked even me. Perhaps the words came from my seventeen-year-old self protecting this now forty-year-old woman. Whoever it was, I love her. Looking my husband in the eyes while sobbing, I firmly stated, "What you did was wrong. I want a divorce. But I will forgive you someday."

The list of people to confront and forgive was long: my husband, mutual friends who became his lovers, people who knew and didn't tell me, and a mom who sold him cocaine in the alley behind our house. Yes, it would be exhausting and time-consuming, but it needed to be done. I couldn't lie and hold on to others' secrets. The toxicity of living inauthentic lives needed to stop.

While driving my son home from practice one night, we pulled into the left turn lane on Pacific Coast Highway and he noticed me crying. I remember this "mom moment" like it was yesterday. Carson was twelve years old at the time, it was a few months after the disclosure, and I worried about him. My son has a deep soul and would never intentionally hurt anyone. This is the same child who screamed at me to stop the car on Valley Drive so he could hand his lunch money to a homeless man on his bike. There was no hiding my pain from his empathy.

"Mom, did Dad cheat on you?" he asked me.

How could I lie to my son? Wouldn't that make me as bad as my husband? At what age do we begin telling our children the truth so they can decipher and learn from their own life experiences? I knew many professionals would disagree with my response, but every cell in my body told me to be honest. Crafting my words, I said, "Honey, Mom is in a lot of pain right now. Your dad hurt my feelings, yes. I won't lie to you and say he didn't cheat on me. He will share with you when the time is right. But trust me, I will be more than fine." We then sat in silence at the stoplight.

"Carson, don't ever lie to or cheat on another person. It's not right. Always be truthful to yourself and others." I could see my son in the rearview mirror. His eyes were sad and he said, "Okay. I'm sorry, Mom."

This was the beginning of speaking my truth to those I loved and cared about. And let me tell you, it hurt. But it's impossible to hold others' pain and lies while maneuvering through your own healing journey. The only way to navigate the mess is to be real and honest. I sobbed the remainder of our way home.

Forgiving is like a twelve-step program that I work on every day, and sometimes I fall off the wagon. When toxic emotions creep in, I remember how good it feels not to live with anger, resentment, and betrayal in my heart. Instead, I choose to keep forgiving, using my five-part process.

Part One: Acknowledge Your Emotions and Feelings

Naturalist Charles Darwin, in his "Evolutionary Theory of Emotion," said that emotions have adapted and evolved to allow both humans and animals to survive and reproduce.[4] We need emotions. They guide us to make decisions and help us process events. But when we stay in our emotions too long, our lives can be endangered.

In the preface, I spoke about the importance of feeling and healing from your traumas. To find forgiveness, you must acknowledge your pain. On my path to healing, I fluctuated many times a day from being an angry, raging woman to a sad, depressed, lonely human curled up in my bathtub, crying. It was like something I had never felt before. My veins were full of poison while my pores oozed hatred and heartache. The experience was both terrifying and exhausting. Not only was I furious about the present, but I was pissed off about my past. My health and relationships were at risk.

The American Psychological Association states that high anger and hostility are associated with an "increased risk of coronary heart disease incidence and mortality, hypertension, blood pressure, and other heart-related problems."[5] And according to *Medical News Today*, depression can lead to fatigue, increased risk of heart disease, chronic pain, autoimmune disorders, and many other health conditions.[6]

Upon learning this information, I thought, *Great, so not only did I lose my marriage, but I could potentially lose my living, breathing life.* Had I not worked on healing, eventually my toxic emotions would have been projected into my most precious commodity: my relationships.

> When you're feeling overwhelmed with an emotion, stop and take time to journal what's triggering you. By noticing what sets off your emotions, you can establish healthy, safe boundaries for your future.
>
> I feel _____ because _____.
>
> What triggered me was _____.

Now let's bring your emotion forward, release it, and find safety. The intention is to quiet your mind, settle into your heart, and align you with your body, mind, and spirit, as well as nature and the present moment. You may find yourself letting go of emotions in ways you least expect, such as through crying or screaming. Whatever happens is okay.

In step one, I shared my favorite meditation for surrendering to peace moments. I used this same meditation to connect with animals and nature every day while in trauma recovery, and we'll use it here as well. As we open our senses to the natural world, we find who we are outside of our pain.

- *Lie on the earth—don't be afraid to get dirty!* Dig your feet into the soil. Sit on a rock next to a creek or riverbed. Or lean up against a tree. Acknowledge the emotions you are feeling within your body.

- *Close your eyes and take a few deep breaths.*
- *Notice what is happening within you as your mind, body, soul, and spirit connects with nature.* Let your mind slow and your shoulders drop while your body sinks into the earth. Don't force anything—just sit or lie in peace.
- *Open your eyes and look around you at this moment. Pick up a piece of nature.* Maybe it's a pine cone, a rock, or a flower. While honoring your feelings and emotions, go even deeper by connecting with nature through your five senses. Be present and "in the now" with what's around you.

  — *Sight:* Take a look at the piece of nature in your hand. Pay attention to the color, details, patterns, and shape.

  — *Sound:* Hold your object to your ear. Does it make any sound when you touch it or move it around?

  — *Smell:* Carefully hold your piece of nature to your nose, close your eyes, and inhale. What does it smell like?

  — *Taste:* Do not taste your object unless you know it is edible.

  — *Touch:* Now touch what is in your hand. How does it feel? Try touching parts of the object and notice where its texture feels different.

Pull out your journal and write about your experience. How did it feel to be lying on the earth and breathing in nature? What shifted or changed within your body while being present with your emotions in nature? Journal what happened within your mind, body, soul, and spirit.

Do this meditation and journaling exercise as many times as needed. This is an organic process that will help lead you to forgiveness.

Part Two: Decide to Forgive

Forgiveness is a choice. We must decide not to exist but to *live* in this world. Once you devote yourself to this way of life, remain committed to the journey. When toxic emotions creep in, use your tools from this book and focus on your intention. It's not easy, and some days are downright hard. But every day will get easier, and the results are worth it.

> I have decided to forgive _____. I made this choice for me.

Your choice to forgive is for you. This is not selfish—it is selfless. Doing this work is hard. By forgiving, you're breaking past patterns, some generational, and welcoming a new, healthy journey.

Part Three: Seek Understanding and Compassion for Those Who Wronged You

To fully embrace forgiveness for the person who caused you pain, step out of your own ego and view your offender through a compassionate lens. Look at their healthy and unhealthy relationships, past experiences, and family unit. Don't be judgmental. Instead, see their history for what it is and notice how their past affected their life. You may be surprised by the compassion you find for people who have experienced turmoil, abuse, traumatic family dynamics, or lack of love.

Think back to the beginning of the book, when I discussed the definition of forgiveness, which doesn't mean excusing the offender's behavior or forgetting it. However, research shows that hurt people have a higher rate of hurting other people. In fact, a study by Dr. Arnon Bentovim and colleagues from London's Institute of Child Health showed that "abused children who came from families where violence was common were more than three times as likely to become abusers as were those who experienced maternal neglect and sexual abuse by females."[7] Forgiveness breaks this chain. By not allowing an offender's pain to hurt you, you're not allowing your pain to hurt others. This process requires a certain amount of courage and vulnerability, both of which can be hard to access after having been traumatized or wronged.

Another way you can actively seek compassion for the person who harmed you is to try to better understand their experiences and perspective.

Seeking to understand and have compassion for those who wronged you isn't an easy task, but it's empowering. Use Michelle's example of trying to find understanding for the woman who killed her sister. It's a powerful reminder of what we're capable of as victims.

In your journal, answer these questions:

- What caused your offender's life to get to this place?
- Were they intentionally trying to hurt you through their actions? Or was this an accident?
- How have their past and present life and relationships affected their behavior toward you?

In addition to this journaling activity, you can seek compassion for the person who harmed you by writing about yourself from his or her perspective. Begin the piece by writing who you are in relation to that person. For instance, if I wrote about myself from my ex-husband's perspective, I would begin with, "Sara is my ex-wife. We were married for seventeen years and had three children." From there, I could write about our courtship, when his life started falling apart, how the behavior affected our marriage and family, the present status of our relationship, and so forth.

The important thing to remember is that you're writing from the other person's perspective. As much as possible, try not to project your own thoughts and feelings onto them. You are viewing their life through a compassionate lens, while understanding what led them to where they are today. Write from your heart, and be honest and authentic.

While the thought of entering your offender's mindset may seem like an impossible, or even undesirable, task, what you can discover about the other person—or about yourself—through this process will enlighten you.

Again, by understanding or finding compassion, you're not pardoning or excusing the person's behavior. Instead, you're saying no to hatred, resentment, and anger, while saying yes to love, kindness, and freedom. This is an important step to come to peace with what happened, while holding your offender accountable for their wrongdoing.

It can be hard when you see others have not, and perhaps are not, learning from their experiences or problems in life—especially if their behaviors continue to hurt you or others. But their journey is not your journey. Trust that they will feel the effect of their actions on their own time. Your job is to view things for what they are and to no longer harbor or hold on to pain. We are blessed to have this opportunity.

Part Four: Hand Back Your Pain, Resentment, and Toxic Emotions Inside of You

In the introduction to this book, I shared how my Catholic Social Services counselor made foster plans for my son without my knowledge or consent. It was devastating to have someone I trusted betray me. I commend my brave seventeen-year-old self for picking up the phone and having a tough conversation. My younger self spoke her truth, handed back outrage, and replaced her hurt with love for her baby.

This experience taught me the importance of letting go of what doesn't serve you. How could I be a good mother if I were living in pain caused by someone else's lack of knowledge and empathy? The system failed me, but I was unwilling to fail my son.

Fast-forward to the age of forty-one, when I was ready to forgive, again. One by one, I made phone calls, sent text and email messages, had personal conversations, and drove six hours to face people who caused anguish and sadness in my life. All of this was due to my husband's transgressions. Within every conversation, I shared how their actions hurt me and that I was no longer holding their pain. Yes, it was exhausting. But more so, it was freeing.

Answer these questions in your journal:

- What emotions and feelings am I handing back to my offender?

- What's the best possible way to confront the person who hurt me?

Can you face the person? Or do you feel most comfortable sending an email or a letter? If the person you're forgiving has died or can't be reached, one option is to imagine them sitting in front of you and having the conversation. Or you can write a letter to that person, read it out loud, and burn the letter afterward.

When I was ready to forgive the man who raped me at seventeen, I couldn't find him. So I imagined he was sitting in front of me, having the conversation. It wasn't any less powerful than when I chose to forgive others in person at the age of forty-one.

- What do I need (that is, personal tools) to complete this step?

Think through what you need to feel safe and prepared while following through with this step. Let me give you an example. When I drove six hours on a Sunday evening to face someone who had relations with my husband, I called my friend in the area, Hilarie, from the car. I shared my plans and asked her to keep her phone on while I confronted this person. She became my safety. For two hours while driving, I rehearsed what I was going to say and how I was going to say it. I imagined what it was going to look like, and I embodied how I would feel. After pulling up to the former friend's house,

I put on my running shoes. Those became my tool to run my body to the door. This person, whom I'd once considered a brother, didn't know I was coming, so the hardest part was not knowing how he'd react. Everything was organic except my plan to hand back pain and forgive.

What happened was beautiful. I calmly spoke my truth, while surrendering how or when it would be received. I still don't know if this man is sorry, but it doesn't matter. I did this for me. He was held accountable for his actions. I handed back my pain, and forgiveness was granted.

- What do I want and need to say?

This is your time to speak and share your truth. Do so wisely.

Here's the script I use. Please alter as you see fit:

"What you did was wrong. And it hurt me. I didn't do anything to deserve this pain. And it's not fair that now I have these toxic feelings living inside of me. I will always remember what happened because that is the truth. But I refuse to let the hurt stay inside of me. Here are all of the feelings that have lived inside of me. They are not good for me. They don't belong to me. I forgive you and harbor no ill will."

This process will look different for everyone. Find what works for you. For example, emotions and feelings are carried in my stomach, or on my shoulders like a heavy backpack. When I hand back my pain, I go through the motion of scooping it from my stomach with my hands, or taking it off of my shoulders like a weight. Does it look weird to the other person? Perhaps. But it visually shows them you're no longer carrying the pain.

Part Five: Fill Your Life with Gratitude and Joy

You have worked hard to let go of so much pain and to forgive. It's time to replace your past toxic thoughts and feelings with gratitude, joy, and love for your future. "Do not complicate your happy life" has been my motto and reminder to find gratitude in simple things: seeing a beautiful rainbow, having grass to lie on, and breathing fresh air.

Brené Brown, research professor and bestselling author, studied the relationship between joy and gratitude. In twelve years of research on eleven thousand pieces of data, she found that every person interviewed who described themselves as joyful also actively practiced gratitude. Brown stated, "Practicing gratitude brings joy into lives."[8]

Using your journal, let's invite gratitude with these practices:

- Start your day in gratitude. Before getting out of bed, ask yourself, *What are five things I'm grateful for?*
- Before eating a meal, say a short prayer: "I am grateful for this food that provides energy for me to live." If you're sitting around a table with family or friends, start a gratitude chain and have everyone share what they are grateful for.

- When dealing with stressful situations, like sitting in traffic or waiting for a difficult meeting at work, take a moment and find gratitude for your breath. Be patient and find self-compassion.
- End your day in gratitude. Before you close your eyes, find five things you're grateful for that day. These can be as simple as wrapping your hands around a hot cup of coffee in the morning or hugging your pet when returning from work.

Now that you're practicing gratitude, fill your life with choices, explore new hobbies, and create happy memories. Welcoming activities you love cultivates joy. If this feels overwhelming because you've never put yourself first, start simple. Do you enjoy taking walks? Baking cookies? Knitting? Writing? Begin with one activity and allow that to guide you. I am grateful for simple things in nature, so it's no wonder I find ultimate joy when hiking mountains and exploring oceans.

Using your journal, answer these questions:

- What do I love to spend time doing?
- When do I feel most happy?
- Where do I find joy?

Give yourself time and space to explore your happiness. Have fun! When trying something new, go back to your personal values from step two and see what you're honoring. Align with your inner warrior, embrace your courage, and step outside of your comfort zone to accomplish things you've been wanting to do.

Life isn't about the experiences that happened *to* you. It's about creating a life you love from the experiences that happened *for* you.

How to Forgive the World

It's easy to be angry at the world when you feel wronged. No one deserves to be judged and condemned by friends, family, or society. That's why I choose to stand up for people like you, me, and others who have experienced loss and trauma and are tired of feeling "less than." You didn't ask for this. Yet I believe that outside of your pain, you have been handed a gift, to share your story and speak out for those who cannot otherwise. The world only knows what it knows. By seeing society through an understanding lens, you and I can teach people how to treat others; educate the courts, judicial system, and others about our traumas; and forgive those who are unaware. Will they all listen? Perhaps not at this moment. Someday, no doubt, they will. The world needs not only my voice but also yours.

For Michelle and her family, it has been difficult to come to terms with how the judicial system handled their case. The woman who hit and killed Angelina was arrested after two days and convicted only of "leaving the scene of an accident," because the authorities didn't have evidence of the woman being under the influence or distracted while driving. She was released after serving less than two weeks due to "overcrowding in jail."

Michelle and her family's deep belief in the judicial system made its betrayal traumatic in and of itself. Michelle said, "My parents are immigrants and it was a big deal for them to become American citizens. Jury duty, voting, and doing your due diligence as a citizen and proud American were necessary in our family. Post the investigation and court hearing, it's been hard to come to terms with how things are processed and how things are investigated based on your economic status or who you are. Things linger in the back of my mind, but I have no control over it, so I try to release it and not hold on to the anger that could otherwise fester inside of me."

We can all be of service in this world. As Michelle told me,

It's so easy to say, "My parents or grandparents were in WWII, and they just shoved it down! Just put it behind you!" But if the world can learn from us healing and putting in the work to process things, they will see their perspective on life can change too.

I never really felt like I had both feet on the ground after Kelvin's death, but now, after doing the work and meditating this past year, sometimes I cry but I can really feel the love from both Kelvin and Angelina, and that's so powerful. I would like for people to know that if you put in the work and put your energy toward that, something good will come from it. Whether that means just for yourself and for your soul, that's good enough.[9]

My entire life, traumas included, has become a gift because of the work I do today. A study from Columbia University suggested that when helping others navigate their stressful situations, we boost our own regulatory skills, thus benefiting our emotional well-being.[10] I can say from experience that this is true. And my hope is that I'm opening doors for you to see the power you have to do the same.

In your journal, answer these questions:

- What does the world need to hear from me?
- By using my story, how can I serve others and make this world a better place?
- How will it feel to speak my truth in the world?
- Where can I share my knowledge? In blogs? A book? In support groups?

In the words of St. Francis of Assisi, "For it is in the giving that we receive."

I'd like to share a beautiful three-part forgiveness meditation for self, others, and the world, which Brittany Lynne and I created for all of you. Please find a quiet, comfortable place—hopefully in nature, but you can also do this at home—where you can listen and receive.

Guided Meditation for Forgiveness

Close your eyes and begin to slow your breath.
Notice what it's like to breathe in and breathe out.
And notice how your body feels right now.
When you think of forgiveness, where in your body do you feel it?
Do you feel relaxed or tense when you think of forgiveness?
Just notice how it feels to invite forgiveness in.
Take a deep inhale.
Release your breath.

As you breathe slowly, allow your body to soften as you invite yourself to move from the space of your head into the space of your heart.

Breathe from your heart space.

Feel your heart begin to open.

As you continue on this journey to release everything that no longer serves you, and invite in the things that you value, feel into the space of your heart.

Breathe in. And release.

Imagine sitting with yourself, either in a mirror or sitting face-to-face. It may be you today or a younger version of yourself. As you look into your own eyes, you see deeper than the surface. See everything you have been through and everything you have experienced. And know that you are doing your best. See yourself without judgment.

As you see yourself, your true self, say to yourself, "I forgive you. I forgive you. I forgive you for everything you have done and held on to. I forgive your past. I forgive your guilt and shame. I forgive you for the ways your actions have affected me. I forgive you. I forgive you. I forgive you."

Allow the image of yourself to slowly fade in your mind, and return to your heart.

Breathe into your heart space.

Inhale.

And exhale.

Now imagine sitting in front of a person who has challenged you. They can be living or may have passed. Forgiveness transcends space and time.

As hard as it might be, sit with this person in front of you
and just notice how you feel.

Imagine looking into their eyes, beyond the surface of who
they are, and see them as another human being.

See everything they have been through and everything
they have experienced. And know that they, too, are
doing their best. See them without judgment.

As you see this person, say to them, "I forgive you. I forgive
you. I forgive you for everything you have done and
held on to. I forgive your past. I forgive your guilt and
shame. I forgive you for the ways your actions have
affected me, and I hand you back my pain. I forgive
you. I forgive you. I forgive you."

As you sit in front of this person and feel your heart getting
lighter, you watch as this person takes a deep breath.
And as they open their mouth to speak, you listen
to their words. And as they speak, you continue to
forgive them.

They say to you, "Thank you for your forgiveness. I accept
your forgiveness. I accept your forgiveness for my guilt
and shame. And for everything I have done that has
affected you. You no longer need to carry what I have
done. You no longer need to carry the past. Or your pain
that you have handed back to me. We are both lighter
for your forgiveness. Thank you for your forgiveness."

Allow the image of this person to slowly fade in your mind,
and return to your heart.

Breathe into your heart space.

Inhale.

And exhale.

Now picture the entire world in your mind. With every
person and creature living on this planet we call home.
This living, breathing organism we all live on.

See everything that every living being has experienced,
in the past and present. And know that we are all
just doing our best. See the entire world without
judgment.

As you see Mother Earth, say to the world, "I send you
forgiveness. I send you forgiveness. I send forgiveness
to everyone and everything that has experienced the
hardships of life on this planet. I send forgiveness for
the past. I send forgiveness for all guilts and shames. I
send forgiveness for all the actions that have affected
others. I send you forgiveness. I send you forgiveness. I
send the entire world forgiveness."

Allow the image of the world to slowly fade in your mind,
and return to your heart. Breathe into your heart space.

Inhale.

And exhale.

As you continue to send forgiveness out into the world,
know that everything is connected. As you give
forgiveness to the world, know that it is pouring back
into you. You deserve the forgiveness that you are so
freely giving to everyone and everything around you.
And as the world around you soaks in the forgiveness
from your heart, say to yourself in your mind:

I surrender to the power of forgiveness.

I know who I am.

I value my worth and I love myself.

I have healthy boundaries for myself and others.

I release judgment of myself and others and continue to show up for myself.

I give myself permission to just be.

I forgive myself.

I forgive those who have wronged me.

I send forgiveness out into the world.

Take another deep breath into your heart space.

And release this breath out into the world.

Begin to bring your awareness back to this moment, back to presence.

As you drop back into your physical body, start to bring gentle movements back to your fingers and toes.

And when you feel ready, begin to open your eyes as you move back into your day with a lighter and forgiving heart.

When you feel comfortable doing so, pick up your journal and free write about your forgiveness journey. Journal everything that comes to you. Let your words flow from your heart, mind, soul, and spirit. It is time. You belong here.

I began this step in honor of all of you for showing up. I'd like to close this step by spreading hope for all those who have caused pain in victims' lives. Including my ex-husband, those friends who betrayed me, so many others who have inflicted pain in my life, and yes, even the man who raped me when I was seventeen.

I pray that you've found reconciliation with the pain that led you to create injustice and hurt others. I hope your recovery leads to forgiveness within yourself. And on behalf of all victims and survivors, I am publicly asking for a favor, to save another innocent soul from becoming a victim: if you have learned from your mistakes, share your knowledge and help create a better world.

All of us—victims, survivors, and offenders alike—have the power to make a difference.

Let's find joy in place of anger.

Kindness in place of hate.

Forgiveness in place of fault.

It's never too late to say, "I am sorry." And it's never too late to say, "I forgive you."

Healing begins with each one of us.

Conclusion

Your Journey Continues

*I*nstead of "conclusion," this section should be called "keep going." I don't want you to stop this forgiveness journey, ever, because it isn't a project that you finish and then move on to something else. It's an ongoing and ever-evolving process to be worked on each day.

Traumas and triggers will continue to occur in life. By welcoming the lifelong forgiveness journey as a gift instead of a dreaded task, you strip yourself of expectations and equip yourself with knowledge and clarity to see life through a lens of truth, love, and hope.

As I've said, I wake in the morning and choose to start my day in forgiveness. I don't have to, but I want to. Plenty of times during my recovery, I found myself in ruminating thoughts of despair, sliding into anger and resentment for being handed a life I never wanted. What mattered was picking myself up and getting back on for the ride, not beating myself up for falling off in the first place. These days became opportunities to examine the cause of my emotions and step more deeply into forgiveness with my past.

If you wake up one day and feel anger toward a person you thought you had forgiven, don't worry. All of your hard work still has value. That's the difference between "I forgave the person who hurt me" and "I'm continuing to forgive the person who hurt me." You don't linger in shame and confusion. It's all about staying on the journey. Let me share ways to know you are on your road to forgiveness:

- YOUR FIRST THOUGHT ABOUT THIS PERSON ISN'T BASED IN SADNESS, RAGE, OR RESENTMENT. When you can look at the person who hurt you through a lens of empathy and understanding, you're on the right path. Seeing them as a human being on his or her own journey is key to detaching from the past and creating your own healthy future. You are no longer defined by what happened but by the learning that came from your deepest pain.

- YOU CHOOSE HOPE FOR THE OTHER PERSON. YOU NO LONGER HOLD A GRUDGE OR WISH THEM ILL WILL. You don't wish this person to be erased from the earth or "want karma to get them back." To make this a better world for all, we need to have hope for others and trust their lives are happening for them too. You believe from your mind, heart, and soul that it's not your job to make sure they learn from their mistakes. You can, however, learn from your own.

- YOU REMEMBER THE GOOD TIMES, NOT JUST THE BAD. As mentioned prior, a mistake turns into a lesson when learning is involved. In place of saying you "wasted your time" with this person—whether a day or a lifetime—you say, "I honor the good moments we had." In my situation, my ex-husband and I had many amazing times together that I'm deeply grateful for.

• YOU CAN HOLD THEM RESPONSIBLE FOR THEIR ACTIONS WHILE BEING KIND. You know your boundaries with this person and accept that they are ever-changing. If or when your boundaries are crossed, you react from a place of love and not ego. In other words, you can take a pause, breathe, and remember that you're in control of your life. It's not about all of the ways this person has wronged you; it's about continuing to choose self-love and self-respect by placing your energy where it is needed—in you. Reset the boundary and move on. Kindness first, always.

• YOU TAKE INVENTORY OF YOUR EMOTIONS AND FIND LOVE, PEACE, AND FREEDOM. Every now and then, close your eyes, place your hands over your heart, be still, and think about this person. Scan your body to see what emotions come up. Do you feel love, peace, and freedom? Or anger, resentment, and sadness? Your body will speak to you; just listen.

About a year into my trauma recovery, I tried to get angry at my former husband for what he'd done. I was on my stand-up paddleboard and thought, *Okay, let's find the anger and let it out.* I had been using my toxic emotions for fuel, and let's face it, my workouts were pretty awesome because of it. So I closed my eyes and tried to access my rage. To my dismay, I couldn't find it. I tried again: *Sara, think about what he did to you! How could he?* Nothing. I

tried conjuring the pictures I found on his phone, the voice
messages and texts from men, but there was nothing. At
that moment, I wasn't angry or sad or full of hate. I realized, for the first time, that my life could again be fueled
by joy, not anger. My forgiveness journey was working.

I wrote this book with three words in mind: *truth*, *inspiration*, and *hope*. They have been my three words for the last six
years, and I want them to be yours too. Find your truth and
speak it from a place of intention and love. Lead an inspired day,
every day. And always have hope for the best life you ultimately
want and deserve. If you feel offtrack, access self-care and bring
yourself back to the definition of forgiveness I presented in the
introduction:

> to acknowledge an offense and the
> consequences of that offense as truth,
> to choose to let go of negative feelings,
> and to cease to harbor animosity toward the offender

We need support for healing and growth in all areas of our
life. If you're ready to continue this journey, please visit my website to access additional resources, learn more ways to grow, and
join our online community, where we dive deeper into self and
life (https://www.saraschultingkranz.com/about-live-boldly/).
Let's have fun together.

Be good to you and keep going—because this world
needs you.

Additional Resources

Nature Healing

Louv, Richard. *The Nature Principle: Reconnecting with Life in a Virtual Age.* Chapel Hill, NC: Algonquin Books, 2012.

Williams, Florence. *The Nature Fix: Why Nature Makes Us Happier, Healthier, and More Creative.* New York: Norton, 2017.

Wohlleben, Peter. *The Hidden Life of Trees: What They Feel, How They Communicate.* Vancouver: Greystone Books, 2016.

Trauma Healing and Psychology

Brown, Brené. *Braving the Wilderness: The Quest for True Belonging and the Courage to Stand Alone.* New York: Random House, 2017.

Brown, Sandra L., with Jennifer R. Young. *Women Who Love Psychopaths: Inside the Relationships of Inevitable Harm with*

Psychopaths, Sociopaths & Narcissists. Balsam Grove, NC: Mask Publishing, 2018.

Orloff, Judith. *Thriving as an Empath: 365 Days of Self-Care for Sensitive People*. Boulder, CO: Sounds True, 2019.

Ortman, Dennis. *Transcending Post-Infidelity Stress Disorder: The Six Stages of Healing*. New York: Celestial Arts, 2009.

Stephens, Barbara, and Marsha Means. *Your Sexually Addicted Spouse: How Partners Can Cope and Heal*. Far Hills, NJ: New Horizon Press, 2009.

Van der Kolk, Bessel. *The Body Keeps the Score: Brain, Mind, and Body in the Healing of Trauma*. New York: Penguin Books, 2015.

Spirituality

Bernstein, Gabrielle. *The Universe Has Your Back: Transform Fear into Faith*. Carlsbad, CA: Hay House, 2016.

Relating to Other Women and Empowerment

Doyle, Glennon. *Love Warrior: A Memoir*. New York: Flatiron Books, 2016.

Doyle, Glennon. *Untamed*. New York: Dial Press, 2020.

Gilbert, Elizabeth. *Big Magic: Creative Living Beyond Fear*. New York: Riverhead Books, 2015.

Gilbert, Elizabeth. *Eat, Pray, Love: One Woman's Search for Everything Across Italy, India, and Indonesia*. New York: Riverhead Books, 2006.

Strayed, Cheryl. *Wild: From Lost to Found on the Pacific Coast Trail*. New York: Vintage Books, 2013.

Acknowledgments

I honor and love all of these beautiful humans for being in my life. Thank you.

My days begin and end with my children, Jacob, Carson, and Christian. A mother's love knows no boundaries. I am so proud of each one of you for becoming who you are today—and for boldly walking on your own journey. Thank you for your trust, for questioning me when needed, and for having tough conversations no child wants to endure. Your bright light will always guide you to your biggest goals and dreams. I believe in you.

To my ex-husband, David. Thank you for being persistent and asking me—your "bus girl"—on our first date. We have many, many happy memories, and regardless of all we have been through together, that is what I choose to focus on. I wish we could go back and lie on Bascom Hill or Library Mall one last time, sharing Rocky Rococo pizza as broke college sweethearts and best friends. If we knew then what we know now, would we still choose this path? I would. Because we have the best kids any parent could ask for. On behalf of them, me, and you, thank you for choosing healthy and becoming who you needed to be.

To Barkley, our rescue dog who rescued us in 2015—we miss you. Thank you for being Bailey's "doggy angel from heaven" and guiding our new tripod, resilient fur baby to our family home. You wiped our tears from above.

To my parents, Jim and Rosie. Thank you for believing (in) me—always—and for putting Jacob first when it seemed as though the world was asking otherwise. Your faith, love, encouragement, dedication, and bravery as parents and grandparents is your legacy. Our kids see you. And now the world sees you. I love you. I love you. I love you.

To my brothers, sisters-in-law, nephews, and niece: Marty, Amy, Milo, Burke, and Adam, and Greg, Jackie, Grace, and Jared. Thank you for accepting and embracing my adventurous spirit and the many ways I've pushed our family limits. To my hero brothers. Thank you for your protection and safety. Our love and joy run deep.

Andrea and Stefanie: my forever BFFs and soul sisters of forty-four and thirty-one years. You are survivors, and when I speak and write, it's for all of us. Thank you for laughter, deep talks, guidance, honesty, makeup tutorials, and cake in bed.

Cocco, Summer, and Grace: no trail, mountain, valley, or ocean would be the same without you. I praise your willingness to do what only us four would attempt. You are all *brave*. Sue and Holly: you will always be my running and karaoke partners. Steve: thank you for putting rocks in my pack. And to my uncle Gene: of the thousands of miles I've hiked in my lifetime, the ones I'll remember most were beside you on our first trip into the Grand Canyon. You are a legend.

Dorit, Dan, and my support group of women: thank you for holding space. You gave me everything I needed to find my courage and voice. I honor you.

Cathy, Andy, Hilarie, and Charlie: not saying anything says everything. Thank you.

My gratitude extends to the team of nine badass women who filmed the documentary *Walk Through This: A Story of Starting Over* in the Grand Canyon over Thanksgiving 2019, during a state of emergency. Together we made (her)story while hiking and filming in sun, rain, wind, rainbows, snow, and a blackout. Thank you, Laura VanZee Taylor, director, cinematographer, and editor, for believing in me and my story. Thank you to Jen Gilomen, cinematographer; Catherine Hood, location sound mixer; Michelle Manson, sherpa; and Brittany Lynne, mindfulness and meditation teacher, for dedicating yourselves to this project. And to these brave women, thank you for sharing your life stories on camera: Hee Soo Chae, Michelle Pinedo, Peggy Witbeck Matheson, and Eliana Moon.

Brittany Lynne, mindfulness and meditation teacher, and Jenna Reiss, breathwork meditation coach: I love you, sisters, for bringing your gifts of healing to the Grand Canyon, and here in this book. Brittany, thank you for consulting beside me in creating the most beautiful meditations to help people heal. You are a true gift. Friends, you can find more of Brittany's meditations on her website, https://brittanylynne.com. Thank you both for walking beside me on this journey.

Beautiful woman, Staci Greason, thank you for your wisdom and guidance while working beside me on my book proposal.

Your dedication and belief in my vision helped get me here today. I love you.

Thank you to my agent, Claudia Cross at Folio Literary Management. I will never forget our phone call on the morning of December 31, 2018. My feet were grounded in wet grass laden with morning dew when I said yes to you.

And to the Harper Horizon team: I never knew a team such as this existed until I met yours. Andrea Fleck-Nisbet, John Andrade, Kayleigh Hines, and my brilliant and patient senior editor, Amanda Bauch: this was a true, dedicated collaboration on many fronts, and I thank you for believing in me. Not too long ago we were strangers. And today, I consider us family. You are all doing beautiful, amazing work in this world. I love you.

To my team and all who have supported me: How could I rise to this space without you? Jo, you are my forever assistant. Pamela, Jordis, Jamie, Ben, and Amber: thank you for keeping the back end together, producing my podcasts, coaching me in business, and being along for this ride.

And to all of my clients, hikers I've met on trails, people I've met in life, and those who continue to guide me on a path of healing: for every moment we've shared, you've made a difference in my life that brought me here today.

We are forever connected, and never, ever alone.

Notes

Introduction

1. Julie Cappiello, "4 Facts about Dolphins That Will Blow Your Mind," *Animals in the Wild* (blog), World Animal Protection, December 4, 2019, https://www.worldanimalprotection.us/blogs/4-facts-about-dolphins.

2. "More Animal Symbolism: Whale Symbolism," Pure Spirit Animal Communication and Training Solutions, accessed April 28, 2020, http://www.pure-spirit.com/more-animal-symbolism/509-whale-symbolism.

3. Jack D. Forbes, "Indigenous Americans: Spirituality and Ecos," *Dædalus* (Fall 2001): 283–300, https://www.amacad.org/sites/default/files/daedalus/downloads/01_fall_daedalus.pdf.

4. Tristan Picotte, "A Native View on Spirit Animals and Animal Medicine," Partnership with Native Americans, August 21, 2018, http://blog.nativepartnership.org/a-native-view-on-spirit-animals-and-animal-medicine/.

5. Forbes, "Indigenous Americans."

6. *Merriam-Webster.com Dictionary*, s.v. "forgive," accessed April 23, 2020, https://www.merriam-webster.com/dictionary/forgive.

Preface

1. American Psychological Association, "Trauma," accessed April 19, 2020, https://www.apa.org/topics/trauma/.

2. National Center for PTSD, "How Common Is PTSD in Adults?," US Department of Veterans Affairs, accessed May 3, 2020, https://www.ptsd.va.gov/understand/common/common _adults.asp.

3. Adolescent Trauma and Substance Abuse Committee, "Understanding the Links Between Adolescent Trauma and Substance Abuse: A Toolkit for Providers," second edition, National Child Traumatic Stress Network, June 2008, https:// www.nctsn.org/sites/default/files/resources//understanding_the _links_between_adolescent_trauma_and_substance_abuse.pdf, 15.

4. National Center for PTSD, "How Common Is PTSD in Adults?"

5. Shaili Jain, "Bracing for an Epidemic of PTSD Among Covid-19 Workers," *Psychology Today*, April 13, 2020, https://www .psychologytoday.com/us/blog/the-aftermath-trauma/202004 /bracing-epidemic-ptsd-among-covid-19-workers.

6. Kirsten Weir, "Grief and COVID-19: Saying Goodbye in the Age of Physical Distancing," April 6, 2020, *Psychology Today*, https://www.apa.org/topics/covid-19/grief-distance.

7. Yuki Noguchi, "Flood of Calls and Texts to Crisis Hotlines Reflects Americans' Rising Anxiety," NPR.org, May 4, 2020, https://www.npr.org/sections/health-shots/2020/05/04 /847841791/flood-of-calls-and-texts-to-crisis-hotlines-reflects -americans-rising-anxiety; Kastalia Medrano, "How to Find a Therapist During the Covid-19 Pandemic," Vox, April 7, 2020, https://www.vox.com/identities/2020/4/7/21207281 /coronavirus-covid-19-how-to-find-a-therapist.

8. Casey L. May and Blair E. Wisco, "Defining Trauma: How

Level of Exposure and Proximity Affect Risk for Posttraumatic Stress Disorder," *Psychological Trauma: Theory, Research, Practice, and Policy* 8, no. 2 (March 2016): 233–40, https://doi:10.1037/tra0000077.

9. Adolescent Trauma and Substance Abuse Committee, "Understanding the Links Between Adolescent Trauma."

10. Christine A. Courtois, "Understanding Complex Trauma, Complex Reactions, and Treatment Approaches," Gift from Within-PTSD Resources for Survivors and Caregivers, accessed May 8, 2020, https://www.giftfromwithin.org/html/cptsd-understanding-treatment.html.

11. Center for Relational Recovery, "Understanding Betrayal Trauma," accessed May 8, 2020, https://www.relationalrecovery.com/understanding-betrayal-trauma/.

12. Michael Samsel, "Trauma Bonding," Abuse and Relationships, accessed April 19, 2020, http://www.abuseandrelationships.org/Content/Survivors/trauma_bonding.html.

13. Suzanne Degges-White, "Love Bombing: A Narcissist's Secret Weapon," *Psychology Today*, April 13, 2018, https://www.psychologytoday.com/us/blog/lifetime-connections/201804/love-bombing-narcissists-secret-weapon.

14. The National Child Traumatic Stress Network, *Domestic Violence and Children: Questions and Answers for Domestic Violence Project Advocates*, November 2010, http://www.doj.state.or.us/wp-content/uploads/2017/08/domestic_violence_and_children.pdf.

15. Bloom for Women, homepage, accessed May 8, 2020, https://bloomforwomen.com/.

16. Randi Gunther, "How Infidelity Causes Post Traumatic Stress Disorder," *Psychology Today*, September 29, 2017, https://www.psychologytoday.com/us/blog/rediscovering-love/201709/how-infidelity-causes-post-traumatic-stress-disorder; Dennis Ortman, *Transcending Post-Infidelity Stress Disorder: The Six Stages of Healing* (New York: Celestial Arts, 2009).

17. Barbara Steffens and Marsha Means, *Your Sexually Addicted*

Spouse: How Partners Can Cope and Heal (Far Hills, NJ: New Horizon Press, 2009), 11.

18. Rachel Goldsmith, Jennifer Freyd, and Anne Deprince, "Betrayal Trauma: Associations with Psychological and Physical Symptoms in Young Adults," *Journal of Interpersonal Violence* 27, no. 3, (October 20, 2011): 547–67, https://doi.org/10.1177/0886260511421672.

19. Patrick Carnes, *Out of the Shadows: Understanding Sexual Addiction* (Center City, MN: Hazelden, 2001), 14.

20. Elizabeth Poth, "Meeting the Crossroad to Recovery: What Is Sex Addiction?," Odonata Wellness Center, April 29, 2020, http://www.odonatawellnesscenter.com/meeting-the-crossroad-to-recovery-what-is-sex-addiction/.

21. The Association of Partners of Sex Addicts and Trauma Specialists, "Betrayal Trauma: Understanding Your Trauma Triggers," February 11, 2016, https://www.apsats.org/2016/02/11/betrayal-trauma-understanding-your-trauma-triggers#:~:text=By%20DrJaniceCaudill%20Trauma%20triggers%20are,places%2C%20things%2C%20or%20situations.&text=Sometimes%20the%20triggers%20are%20obvious,like%20sex%20scenes%20in%20movies.

22. Matthew Dahlitz and the Science of Psychotherapy (SoP), "The Triune Brain," October 26, 2016, https://www.thescienceofpsychotherapy.com/the-triune-brain/.

23. Bessel van der Kolk, *The Body Keeps the Score* (New York: Penguin, 2015), 59.

24. Anna Aslanian, "Betrayal Trauma in Addiction," the Gottman Institute, October 21, 2019, https://www.gottman.com/blog/betrayal-trauma-in-addiction/.

25. Aslanian.

26. James Hopper and David Lisak, "Why Rape and Trauma Survivors Have Fragmented and Incomplete Memories," *TIME*, December 9, 2014, https://time.com/3625414/rape-trauma-brain-memory/.

27. van der Kolk, *The Body Keeps the Score*, 53.

28. van der Kolk, 73.

29. van der Kolk, 73.

30. Brian Clark Howard, "Connecting with Nature Boosts Creativity and Health," *National Geographic*, June 30, 2013, https://www.nationalgeographic.com/news/2013/6/130628 -richard-louv-nature-deficit-disorder-health-environment /#close; Richard Louv, "What Is Nature-Deficit Disorder?," RichardLouv.com, October 15, 2019, http://richardlouv.com /blog/what-is-nature-deficit-disorder/.

31. Louv, "What Is Nature-Deficit Disorder?"

32. van der Kolk, *The Body Keeps the Score*, 73.

33. "Somatic Therapy," *Psychology Today*, accessed May 22, 2020, https://www.psychologytoday.com/us/therapy-types/somatic -therapy.

34. U.S. Environmental Protection Agency, "Report on the Environment: Indoor Air Quality," EPA.gov, last updated July 16, 2018, https://www.epa.gov/report-environment/indoor -air-quality; "Brain Post: How Much Time Does the Average American Spend Outdoors?," SnowBrains, March 9, 2020, https://snowbrains.com/brain-post-much-time-average -american-spend-outdoors/.

35. "How Much Screen Time Is Too Much?," Scripps.org, February 22, 2019, https://www.scripps.org/news_items/6626 -how-much-screen-time-is-too-much.

36. Kristen Rogers, "US Teens Use Screens More Than Seven Hours a Day on Average—and That's Not Including School Work," CNN.com, October 29, 2019, https://www.cnn.com /2019/10/29/health/common-sense-kids-media-use-report -wellness/index.html.

37. Jon Henley, "Richard Louv: Let Them Climb Trees," *Guardian*, June 4, 2010, https://www.theguardian.com/lifeandstyle/2010 /jun/05/nature-deficit-disorder-richard-louv.

38. Matej Mikulic, "Total Number of Medical Prescriptions

Dispensed in the U.S. from 2009 to 2018," Statista, November 8, 2019, https://www.statista.com/statistics/238702/us-total -medical-prescriptions-issued/.

39. Rebecca Ahrnsbrak et al., "Key Substance Use and Mental Health Indicators in the United States: Results from the 2016 National Survey on Drug Use and Health," U.S. Department of Health and Human Services, Substance Abuse and Mental Health Services Administration, September 2017, https://www .samhsa.gov/data/sites/default/files/NSDUH-FFR1-2016 /NSDUH-FFR1-2016.pdf.

40. "Prescription Opioid Data," CDC.gov, last updated March 12, 2020, https://www.cdc.gov/drugoverdose/data/prescribing.html ?CDC_AA_refVal=https%3A%2F%2Fwww.cdc.gov %2Fdrugoverdose%2Fdata%2Foverdose.html.

41. Cora Peterson et al., "Suicide Rates by Industry and Occupation—National Violent Death Reporting System, 32 States, 2016," *MMWR and Morbidity and Mortality Weekly Report* 69, no. 3 (January 24, 2020): 57–62, http://dx.doi.org /10.15585/mmwr.mm6903a1.

42. World Health Organization, "Constitution," WHO.int, accessed April 19, 2020, https://www.who.int/about/who-we-are /constitution.

43. Robin Mejia, "Green Exercise May Be Good for Your Head," *Environmental Science & Technology* 44, no. 10 (May 15, 2010): 3469, https://doi.org/10.1021/es101129n.

44. Jason Mark, "Get Out of Here: Scientists Examine the Benefits of Forests, Birdsong, and Running Water," *New York Times*, March 2, 2017, https://www.nytimes.com/2017/03/02/books /review/nature-fix-florence-williams.html.

45. Florence Williams, *The Nature Fix: Why Nature Makes Us Happier, Healthier, and More Creative* (New York: Norton, 2017), 43–44.

46. Williams, 30.

47. Williams, 47.

48. Carolyn Gregoire, "The New Science of the Creative Brain on Nature," *Outside*, March 18, 2016, https://www.outsideonline.com/2062221/new-science-creative-brain-nature.

49. Gregoire.

50. Gregoire.

51. Williams, *The Nature Fix*, 48.

52. Williams, 49.

53. Gregoire, "The New Science."

54. Kirstie Pursey, "Everything Is Energy and Science Has Proved It—Here Is How," Learning Mind, December 13, 2017, https://www.learning-mind.com/everything-is-energy/.

55. "The Complete Guide to the 7 Chakras—For Beginners," *Mindvalley* (blog), December 17, 2017, https://blog.mindvalley.com/7-chakras/?utm_source=blog.

56. "The Complete Guide to the 7 Chakras"; "What Are the 7 Chakras?," Yoga International, accessed April 23, 2020, https://yogainternational.com/article/view/what-are-the-7-chakras.

57. "What Are the 7 Chakras?"

58. Peter Wohlleben, *The Hidden Life of Trees: What They Feel, How They Communicate* (Vancouver: Greystone Books, 2016), 96.

59. Ruth Raanaas, Grete Patil, and Terry Hartig, "Health Benefits of a View of Nature through the Window: A Quasi-Experimental Study of Patients in a Residential Rehabilitation Center," *Clinic Rehabilitation* 26, no. 1 (January 2012): 21–32, https://doi: 10.1177/0269215511412800; Jacob Benfield, B. Derrick Taff, Peter Newman, and Joshua Smyth, "Natural Sound Facilitates Mood Recovery," *Ecopsychology* 6, no. 3 (September 19, 2014): 183–88, https://doi.org/10.1089/eco.2014.0028.

Step 1: Set Your Intention and Surrender

1. Yasmin Anwar, "Nature Is Proving to Be Awesome Medicine for PTSD," Berkeley News, July 18, 2018, https://news.berkeley.edu/2018/07/12/awe-nature-ptsd/.

2. Brian Wansink and Jefferey Sobal, "Mindless Eating: The 200 Daily Food Decisions We Overlook," *Environment and Behavior* 39, no 1 (January 2017): 106–23, https://doi.org/10.1177 /0013916506295573.

3. "Calling All Angels," Train, *My Private Nation*, Columbia Records, 2003.

4. Kyle Gray, "The Universe Is Recruiting You! Kyle Gray Explains Angel Numbers and Signs from Above," Heal Your Life, April 11, 2016, https://www.healyourlife.com/the-universe-is -recruiting-you-kyle-gray-explains-angel-numbers-and-signs -from-above.

5. In text message communication and phone conversation with the author on January 14, 2020.

Step 2: Ask, "Who Am I?"

1. Mihir Zaveri and Emily Rueb, "How Many Animals Have Died in Australia's Wildfires?," *New York Times*, January 11, 2020, https://www.nytimes.com/2020/01/11/world/australia/fires -animals.html.

2. Bill Chappell and Merrit Kennedy, "U.S. Charges Dozens of Parents, Coaches in Massive College Admissions Scandal," NPR.org, March 12, 2019, https://www.npr.org/2019/03/12 /702539140/u-s-accuses-actresses-others-of-fraud-in-wide -college-admissions-scandal.

3. Sara Schulting Kranz, "We Need a New Definition of Forgiveness," TEDx Manhattan Beach, uploaded January 15, 2020, https://youtu.be/xIU2HavaGf0.

4. Reaca Pearl, "11 Things That Will Help You Hold Space for Someone," *GoodTherapy* (blog), May 23, 2017, https://www .goodtherapy.org/blog/11-things-that-will-help-you-hold-space -for-someone-0523175.

5. This quote is usually attributed to Mahatma Gandhi.

6. While often attributed to Albert Einstein, the original source of this quote is debated.

7. In email communication and phone conversations with the author, spring 2018.

Step 3: Embrace Self-Worth + Self-Love

1. "Amazing Heart Facts," from *Cut to the Heart*, Nova, originally aired April 8, 1997, https://www.pbs.org/wgbh/nova/heart/heartfacts.html.
2. Harvard Women's Health Watch, "Takotsubo Cardiomyopathy (Broken-Heart Syndrome)," Harvard Health Publishing, last updated January 29, 2020, https://www.health.harvard.edu/heart-health/takotsubo-cardiomyopathy-broken-heart-syndrome.
3. Association for Psychological Science, "Can Fetus Sense Mother's Psychological State? Study Suggests Yes," ScienceDaily, November 10, 2011, https://www.sciencedaily.com/releases/2011/11/111110142352.htm.
4. Diana Divecha, "Can a Pregnant Woman's Experience Influence Her Baby's Temperament?," Developmental Science, October 8, 2018, https://www.developmentalscience.com/blog/2018/10/1/can-a-pregnant-womans-experience-influence-her-babys-temperament; see also Elizabeth A. Werner et al., "Prenatal Predictors of Infant Temperament," *Developmental Psychobiology* 49, no. 5 (June 18, 2007): 474–84, https://doi.org/10.1002/dev.20232.
5. Divecha.
6. Dr. Martin Luther King Jr., "What Is Your Life's Blueprint?," *Seattle Times*, accessed April 27, 2020, https://projects.seattletimes.com/mlk/words-blueprint.html.

Step 4: Set Boundaries for Yourself

1. Sara Schulting Kranz, "We Need a New Definition of Forgiveness," TEDx Manhattan Beach, uploaded January 15, 2020, https://youtu.be/xIU2HavaGf0.
2. Samantha Vicenty, "How to Block Every Type of Energy Vampire," *O: The Oprah Magazine*, October 31, 2019, https://

www.oprahmag.com/life/relationships-love/a29623497/energy
-vampires/.

3. Stephanie A. Sarkis, "11 Warning Signs of Gaslighting,"
Psychology Today, January 22, 2017, https://www
.psychologytoday.com/us/blog/here-there-and-everywhere
/201701/11-warning-signs-gaslighting.

4. Vicenty, "How to Block Every Type of Energy Vampire."

5. Vicenty.

6. Vicenty.

7. Vicenty.

8. Vicenty.

9. Vicenty.

Step 5: Persevere When the Work Becomes Hard

1. Nadia Kounang, "What Is the Science Behind Fear?," CNN.com,
October 29, 2015, https://www.cnn.com/2015/10/29/health
/science-of-fear/index.html; also see Eleanor J. Gibson and
Richard D. Walk, "The 'Visual Cliff,'" *Scientific American* 202,
no. 4 (1960): 67–71, https://www.jstor.org/stable/24940447.

2. Daphne Davis and Jeffrey Hayes, "What Are the Benefits of
Mindfulness?," APA.org, July–August 2012, https://www.apa
.org/education/ce/mindfulness-benefits.pdf.

3. Davis and Hayes, "What Are the Benefits of Mindfulness?";
J. W. Hughes, D. M. Fresco, R. Myerscough, M. H. M. van
Dulmen, L. E. Carlson, and R. Josephson, "Randomized
Controlled Trial of Mindfulness-Based Stress Reduction for
Prehypertension," *Psychosomatic Medicine* 75, no. 8 (October
2013): 721–28, https://doi.org/10.1097/PSY.0b013e3182a3e4e5.

4. Jamie Ballard, "A Third of Americans Know Someone Who
Has Died by Suicide," YouGov, September 13, 2018, https://
today.yougov.com/topics/lifestyle/articles-reports/2018/09/13
/americans-depression-suicide-mental-health.

5. Daniel Stevens et al., "Posttraumatic Stress Disorder Increases
Risk for Suicide Attempt in Adults with Recurrent Major

Depression," *Depression & Anxiety* 30, no. 10 (October 2013): 940–46, https://doi.org/10.1002/da.22160.

6. Nicholas Tarrier and Lynsey Gregg, "Suicide Risk in Civilian PTSD Patients," *Social Psychiatry and Psychiatric Epidemiology* 39 (August 2004): 655–61, https://doi.org/10.1007/s00127-004 -0799-4.

Step 6: *Do Less* + *Be* More

1. "Head, Heart, and Gut: The Three Brains That Control Our Intuition," *Invisible Edge* (blog), accessed March 19, 2020, https://invisible-edgellc.com/head-heart-gut/.

2. HeartMath Institute, *Science of the Heart: Exploring the Role of the Heart in Human Performance*, vol. 1 (1993–2001), accessed March 19, 2020, https://www.heartmath.org/resources/downloads /science-of-the-heart/.

3. HeartMath Institute.

4. HeartMath Institute.

5. "Meditation Statistics: Unveiling Our Meditation Habits," TheGoodBody.com, June 24, 2019, https://www.thegoodbody .com/meditation-statistics/.

6. Belle Beth Cooper, "What Happens to the Brain When You Meditate," Lifehacker, August 26, 2013, https://lifehacker.com /what-happens-to-the-brain-when-you-meditate-and-how-it -1202533314.

7. Florence Williams, *The Nature Fix: Why Nature Makes Us Happier, Healthier, and More Creative* (New York: Norton, 2017), 25.

8. Drake Baer, "Here's How Zen Meditation Changed Steve Jobs' Life and Sparked a Design Revolution," *Business Insider*, January 5, 2019, https://www.businessinsider.com/steve-jobs-zen -meditation-buddhism-2015-1.

9. Steve Jobs, "'You've Got to Find What You Love,' Jobs Says," speech transcript, Stanford News, June 14, 2005, https://news .stanford.edu/2005/06/14/jobs-061505/.

10. Sentinel and Enterprise Contributor, "All Items Hold Energy of

Previous Owner," Sentinel & Enterprise, last updated July 11, 2019, https://www.sentinelandenterprise.com/2017/11/28/all-items-hold-energy-of-previous-owner/.

Step 7: Practice Forgiveness

1. In a videoconference interview with the author, March 25, 2020.
2. Scott R. Braithwaite, Edward A. Selby, and Frank D. Fincham, "Forgiveness and Relationship Satisfaction: Mediating Mechanisms," *Journal of Family Psychology* 25, no. 4 (August 2011): 551–59, https://doi.org/10.1037/a0024526.
3. In a videoconference interview with the author, March 25, 2020.
4. John Black, "Darwin in the World of Emotions," *Journal of the Royal Society of Medicine* 95, no. 6 (June 2002): 311–13, https://doi.org/10.1177/014107680209500617.
5. Deborah Smith, "Angry Thoughts, At-Risk Hearts," *Monitor on Psychology* 34, no. 3 (March 2003): 46, https://www.apa.org/monitor/mar03/angrythoughts.
6. Zawn Villines, "How Does Depression Affect the Body?," *Medical News Today*, July 9, 2018, https://www.medicalnewstoday.com/articles/322395.
7. Salynn Boyles, "Do Sexually Abused Kids Become Abusers?," WebMD, February 6, 2003, https://www.webmd.com/mental-health/news/20030206/do-sexually-abused-kids-become-abusers#1.
8. Brené Brown, "Brené Brown on Joy and Gratitude," Global Leadership Network, November 21, 2008, https://globalleadership.org/articles/leading-yourself/brene-brown-on-joy-and-gratitude/.
9. In a videoconference interview with the author, March 25, 2020.
10. Bruce P. Doré, "Helping Others Regulate Emotion Predicts Increased Regulation of One's Own Emotions and Decreased Symptoms of Depression," *Personality and Social Psychology Bulletin* 43, no. 5 (March 20, 2017): 729–39, https://doi.org/10.1177/0146167217695558.

About the Author

S ara Schulting Kranz is a professional life and leadership coach, motivational speaker, and certified wilderness guide. She specializes in helping those who have suffered hardship or trauma to find forgiveness and strength in their lives through one-on-one coaching and guided wilderness retreats in locations such as the Grand Canyon and the Pacific Rim. A documentary of Sara's healing journey in nature is currently in production, with an expected release date of fall 2021. *Walk Through This: A Story of Starting Over* was filmed in Black Earth, Wisconsin; Los Angeles, California; and with ten women in the Grand Canyon. You can be a part of or learn more about this film, created by Laura VanZee Taylor, here: www.walkthroughthis.com. Laura's first feature-length documentary, *I Am Maris*, is now available on Netflix.

When not in the mountains, on the Pacific Ocean, or hanging out with her sons, you can find Sara through her website and on her social media links:

Website: https://www.saraschultingkranz.com/
Instagram: https://www.instagram.com/saraschultingkranz/
Facebook: https://www.facebook.com/sara.schultingkranz
Facebook: https://www.facebook.com/liveboldly/

Please reach out and share your forgiveness journey thoughts. For coaching, retreat, or speaking inquiries, please email: sara@saraschultingkranz.com or jo@saraschultingkranz.com.